PHYSICAL EDUCATION
ACTIVITIES SERIES

LACROSSE
FOR
GIRLS and WOMEN

ANNE LEE DELANO
Bryn Mawr College

WM. C. BROWN COMPANY PUBLISHERS
DUBUQUE, IOWA

BROWN

PHYSICAL EDUCATION ACTIVITIES SERIES

Consulting Editor:

AILEENE LOCKHART
University of Southern California
Los Angeles, California

Evaluation Materials Editor:

JANE A. MOTT
Smith College
Northampton, Massachusetts

Copyright © 1970 by
Wm. C. Brown Company Publishers

ISBN 0—697—07018—2

Printed in the United States of America

ARCHERY, *Wayne C. McKinney*
BADMINTON, *Margaret Varner Bloss*
BADMINTON, ADVANCED, *Wynn Rogers*
BASKETBALL FOR MEN, *Glenn Wilkes*
BASKETBALL FOR WOMEN, *Frances Schaafsma*
BIOPHYSICAL VALUES OF MUSCULAR ACTIVITY, *E. C. Davis, Gene A. Logan, and Wayne C. McKinney*
BOWLING, *Joan Martin*
CANOEING AND SAILING, *Linda Vaughn and Richard Stratton*
CIRCUIT TRAINING, *Robert P. Sorani*
CONDITIONING AND BASIC MOVEMENT CONCEPTS, *Jane A. Mott*
CONTEMPORARY SQUARE DANCE, *Patricia A. Phillips*
FENCING, *Muriel Bower and Torao Mori*
FIELD HOCKEY, *Anne Delano*
FIGURE SKATING, *Marion Proctor*
FOLK DANCE, *Lois Ellfeldt*
GOLF, *Virginia L. Nance and E. C. Davis*
GYMNASTICS FOR MEN, *A. Bruce Frederick*
GYMNASTICS FOR WOMEN, *A. Bruce Frederick*
HANDBALL, *Michael Yessis*
ICE HOCKEY, *Don Hayes*
JUDO, *Daeshik Kim*
KARATE AND PERSONAL DEFENSE, *Daeshik Kim and Tom Leland*
LACROSSE FOR GIRLS AND WOMEN, *Anne Delano*
MODERN DANCE, *Esther E. Pease*
RACQUETBALL/PADDLEBALL, *Philip E. Allsen and Alan Witbeck*
PHYSICAL AND PHYSIOLOGICAL CONDITIONING FOR MEN, *Benjamin Ricci*
RUGBY, *J. Gavin Reid*
SKIING, *Clayne Jensen and Karl Tucker*
SKIN AND SCUBA DIVING, *Albert A. Tillman*
SOCCER, *Richard L. Nelson*
SOCCER AND SPEEDBALL FOR WOMEN, *Jane A. Mott*
SOCIAL DANCE, *William F. Pillich*
SOFTBALL, *Marian E. Kneer and Charles L. McCord*
SQUASH RACQUETS, *Margaret Varner Bloss and Norman Bramall*
SWIMMING, *Betty J. Vickers and William J. Vincent*
SWIMMING, ADVANCED, *James A. Gaughran*
TABLE TENNIS, *Margaret Varner Bloss and J. R. Harrison*
TAP DANCE, *Barbara Nash*
TENNIS, *Joan Johnson and Paul Xanthos*
TENNIS, ADVANCED, *Chet Murphy*
TRACK AND FIELD, *Kenneth E. Foreman and Virginia L. Husted*
TRAMPOLINING, *Jeff T. Hennessy*
VOLLEYBALL, *Glen H. Egstrom and Frances Schaafsma*
WEIGHT TRAINING, *Philip J. Rasch*
WRESTLING, *Arnold Umbach and Warren R. Johnson*

2/75

Contents

Preface

In the hope that this game will be learned by more people and better understood and enjoyed by participants and spectators alike, the writing of this book was undertaken. Although the number of players and teachers is increasing each year the value and challenge of lacrosse are still not well known in this country, and therefore, not fully appreciated. It would be wise to mention that both the teacher and the players can "make or break" any game, for a game is judged by their attitudes and their performances. An exposition of the challenge of the skills involved; their execution within the game; the thoughtfulness, the initiative and the cooperation necessary to play lacrosse well, has been attempted within the allotted pages in this book. The presentation is for the beginner or the person with only a little knowledge of lacrosse. No single book could convey all the aspects of the game. Its possibilities and its freedom will be appreciated only as the result of practice and play. Control of one's own body and crosse, plus consideration for others playing with and against you will determine the effectiveness of the play and the pleasure that the game should give to players and spectators alike.

The necessary techniques, the requirements of each position and the basic fundamentals of attack and defense play are included here. Added also are self evaluation questions and suggestions for some simple practices to do with a partner or partners. The keen player will evolve for herself further practices and pose more difficult questions involving more complex groupings and understandings with more challenging emphasis, as ability increases.

The reward for writing this book will be enough if it helps in some small way to develop a greater understanding of this delightful game, if it increases the zest and the fun it should provide, and if it improves the skills which are necessary for good play. The demands of lacrosse make it a challenging, unique and delightful team sport for girls and women.

Self-evaluation questions are distributed throughout this text. These pertain to knowledge, skill, understanding and application. These questions are samples which should give the reader an idea of the kinds of understandings and abilities she should be acquiring in order to develop mastery of this sport. The reader should respond to these questions carefully and should attempt to devise additional ones to stimulate and evaluate her learnings.

1

The Game

"What's in a name?" seems an appropriate question with which to open this book. The name lacrosse has perhaps been detrimental to its growth as a game for girls. Either the sport is completely unknown, or, if known, is associated only with men's participation; theirs is a game of hard and sometimes rough play with a great deal of body contact. "For Girls and Women," added here, should immediately convey to the uninformed that there is enough difference to warrant a separate book. Actually, the only similarity between the two games is that each is played with a "crosse" and a hard rubber ball. The lacrosse sticks which girls use are all similar in size and weight, whereas in the men's game the length, weight and size of the crosse depend upon the position of attack, defense or goalkeeper and the crosses have deep pockets. Whereas the men wear helmets, faceguards, gauntlets and armguards, the only player in women's lacrosse who needs to wear extra protection is the goalkeeper; she is attired in a chest protector, goalpads, like those worn in field hockey, and usually a face mask similar to a softball catcher's mask.

Lacrosse is the most beautiful team sport that girls play, because of its grace and flow of movement. Lacrosse is an aerial game based on the natural abilities of running, throwing, catching, twisting and dodging, and is the "fastest team game on two feet." No other sport can claim such freedom of movement, for it is unrestricted by boundaries other than natural barriers or those mutually decided upon ahead of time; play goes on even behind the goal. The few rules are concerned with the safety and control of the game. Its very freedom sets or imposes its own limitations. With no offside rule, very few field markings to inhibit the player and her movements, and no specific set areas of play for either attack or defense, the game requires initiative, quick thinking and reaction, and a superb physical and mental interplay among all the participants.

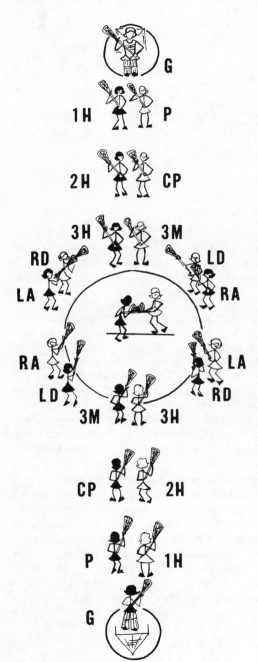

Lacrosse is similar to basketball but on a much larger scale of play. The passing, the weaving, the feinting to move the ball toward the goal involve the same basic elements. The lining up to begin the game is almost unique; only in basketball and lacrosse are the players positioned from goal to goal instead of being separated by the center line, (Diagram 1).

A team is composed of twelve players: *the six attack players are first home, second home, third home, left attack wing, right attack wing and center; the six defense players are goalkeeper, point, cover point, third man, left defense wing and right defense wing.* The teams line up with first homes nearest the goal they are attacking and points nearest to the goal they are defending. Another look at the diagram will help you to learn which defense player marks which attack player.

You will also note the three circles on the field. The center circle imposes a restriction on the players only at the beginning of each half and after each goal is scored, and the restriction lasts only until the ball is in play. The circle around each goal is known as the *crease*. The crease is for

Figure 1—The Center Draw

2

the protection of the goalkeeper as it places a distance barrier between the person who shoots and the goal. No player may have any part of her body or her crosse over the crease before, during, or after her shot for goal.

The game is started by a *draw*. The ball is placed between the backs of the two crosses of the centers and upon command from the umpire *"Ready, draw"*, the players move their crosses upwards and outwards with the correct amount of pressure to send the ball to one of their attacks—usually the left wing. As soon as the ball is in the air, all players begin to move where they wish, using their ingenuity and originality to make spaces, to draw their defenses and to make themselves available to receive a pass as they move into a space. Constant alertness for moves by other members of their team, space awareness to avoid crowding, and the ability to catch and throw while moving at top speed characterize the game. *Man-to-man marking* is characteristic of the defense.

While watching or playing lacrosse one cannot help but be impressed with the flow of the game and its freedom from constant whistling by the umpire, caused by either line violations or fouling. *Fouls* are charging or pushing, uncontrolled checking of an opponent's crosse in attempting to dislodge the ball, or interfering with the crosse of a player who does not have possession of the ball. When the whistle does blow, all players must stand and may not move to reposition themselves until the umpire says "play". Should a player be fouled, she is awarded a *free position* which means she is given the ball and all other players must be five yards from her. On the word "play", she may run, throw or shoot as she chooses. Should two opponents foul each other, a *draw* is taken on the spot by the two players involved. Neither a free position nor a draw may be taken within ten yards of the goal. Should the ball go over the designated boundaries, the ball is put in play either by the player closest to it at the time of the whistle or by a *throw-on* between the two players nearest the ball at the time. One point is awarded for each goal and a full game consists of two twenty-five minute halves.

In this brief discussion, you will have become aware of the rather unique names of the positions and the unfamiliar terms such as *draw, free position* and *throw-on* or *throw-in*. In the chapters which follow, positions and their responsibilities, as well as terminologies used in the game will be more fully discussed. Suffice for the moment to reiterate that lacrosse is a game without equal in its freedom of thought and movement, unhampered by set plays and with logical, clear and obvious rules. The game in its finest form suggests the grace and beauty of dance forms, involving upright, stretching, twisting and flowing movement, performed at top speed, for the ball can cover the field and change direction rapidly between the two goals which are one hundred yards apart. The quick change from attack to defense and vice-versa, requires alertness, constant concentration, and complete empathy and understanding among the twelve players who comprise a team.

2

Basic Techniques

Before you have practiced all the techniques described here, you will have probably tried the game. Having had this experience, the reason for practicing and perfecting the following techniques should become both obvious and challenging. These techniques are few and their correlation of movement is gratifying to explore, to feel and to perform. It would be wrong not to admit that there will be moments of frustration when the ball seems reluctant to stay in your crosse while you are running, when it bounces out of your crosse as you try to catch it, when you struggle to get the ball off the ground while harried by an opponent. As you observe others who have already achieved success, your feeling of inadequacy may be intensified for it all looks so simple. Remember that this is a sign of perfection and the relaxation and grace of the movement have become a part of the performer. Your first efforts will perhaps produce just the opposite—tension and a feeling of awkwardness. Relaxation and grace of movement will come quite easily to some, to others it will take more time but the end result cannot be measured by your first efforts at learning this new and very exhilerating and exciting game. From the very beginning do your stickwork *on the move* with as much speed as possible, for speed of foot will help to achieve the necessary quickness of [the] movement and develop your endurance for the games to follow.

What You Wear is important. A tunic, short skirt or shorts with good leg room will provide freedom in running, bending and stretching and will also add to the effect of gracefulness. You should wear rubber cleated shoes for these assist tremendously in obtaining a quick getaway, and make it possible for you to change direction quickly.

Your Lacrosse Stick, referred to from now on as your "crosse", is a very precious piece of equipment, usually handmade and very durable if properly taken care of. The length and weight of all crosses are fairly simi-

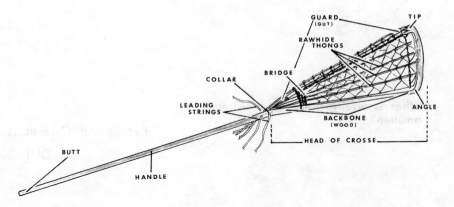

Figure 2—The Crosse

lar, though some are better balanced than others. You will begin to feel this as you become more familiar with crosses and as you attempt to throw and catch. The weight should be slightly toward the wood side. Where the wood bends is known as the *angle* and this shape has been obtained by steaming the wood. The angle, therefore, is a vulnerable part of your crosse and must be protected from undue stress and strain. *Never* lean on your crosse. Opposite the wooden side or backbone of the crosse is the *guard.* When taut, it provides a firm barrier opposite the wood and thereby completes the playing surface of the crosse known as the *pocket.* The guard is made taut by tightening the rawhide thongs attached to each of the strips of gut used in making the guard. Tighten the thongs in such a way that they can be easily released when you finish playing, for if not loosened the constant stress will begin to break down the angle. Where guard and wood meet at the narrowest point of the pocket is the *throat,* and to prevent the ball from becoming lodged in such a narrow space, you will find another bit of gut woven across and this is the *bridge.* The end of the crosse is called the *butt.* (Figure 2)

THE GRIP. Place the crosse flat on the ground, the butt end toward you, pocket facing upward. Place the hand of your throwing arm at the throat of the crosse, matching the V formed by your thumb and forefinger to the V shape of the crosse, letting your thumb lightly meet your forefinger or third finger with the other fingers firmly but gently around the crosse. With fingers slightly spread, pick up the crosse so that your hand is forehead height or slightly higher. The forearm should be dropped along the shaft of the crosse; this will remove tension in the grip, the arm and the shoulder. Then grip the butt end of the crosse naturally with the other hand. The bottom hand should be waist height at least. *As the bottom*

5

What is wrong with this cradling position?

Evaluation Questions

CRADLING

hand initiates all movements of the crosse, the grip must be firm. A hand dropped below waist height cannot grip completely; therefore, the bottom hand must always move at waist height, or above, in all the actions of the crosse. The grip of the bottom hand aways remains the same and the grip of the top hand changes slightly *only* with the shoulder pass or over-arm throw or with the overarm shot. The top hand grip should be firm but gentle, enough to control the crosse and yet allow freedom of action for the wrist which moves with a rotating inward, outward action. (Figure 3)

Note: *As the majority of people are right handed and therefore play right hand up, all explanations in this book are described for the right-hander; should you play left hand up, just reverse the direction yourself.*

The crosse now held as explained, should be perpendicular to the ground, one hand below the other, the forearm of the lower arm dictating the distance from the body, and the forearm of the top arm resting against the shaft of the crosse. From the start, remember to keep the crosse moving in the same axis as the body.

Perhaps as you are introduced to this sport you may be given a ball, told to put it into your crosse and then to run as fast as you can changing direction every so often, while

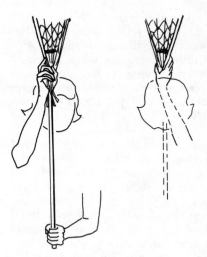

Figure 3—The Grip

Diagram A:

CRADLING

WRONG

trying to keep the ball in the crosse. Should you drop it, pick it up with your crosse while still running, remembering to keep your hands placed as they were when you started.

Some of you will have managed to retain possession of the ball while others will have lost it fairly often. Also some will have been able to pick up the ball quite easily, while others chased it merrily along the ground, or kept losing it as they brought the crosse into a more vertical position. All these results can be expected since they are the natural outcome of beginning efforts.

Next you will undoubtedly be shown how to "ask" for the ball: point your crosse into the space or in the direction you want to receive the ball as you run, making sure that the pocket of your crosse is behind the flight of the ball as it comes. Your partner will try to throw the ball from her crosse to yours while she too is running. Once again immediate success will come to some and undoubtedly slight frustration to others. [But] is this not true in everything we learn? [Remember] the results of these first attempts are not indicative of your potential skill or enjoyment.

CRADLING. This term describes the movement of the crosse while you are in possession of the ball. Simultaneous swinging of the arms from side to side combined with the correct movement of the wrists, sets up a type centrifugal force which keeps the crosse "wrapped around" the ball so that it cannot fall out regardless of which way you may twist, turn or move. The theory is similar to taking a pail of water and swinging it around and around; if this action is even, no water is lost. The term "cradling" also denotes *smooth* action. If you were successful in maintaining possession of the ball in the beginning while trying to move your crosse more or less perpendicular to the ground, your cradling action had already begun, as your arms moved quite rhythmically with your running. It is an inherent

7

Figure 4—Cradling

action. However, to prevent frustration later on when you must deal with an opponent intent upon robbing you of the ball and you must move your crosse close to your body from side to side as you try to dodge by her, it is important to perfect this very basic technique. You will discover that this same movement is similar to that used in performing the *pivot turn*, the *dodge* and the *shoulder pass*. Perhaps there is no other sport in which the basic movement is so absolutely tied together with the majority of the skills important to the game.

Having checked your grip again, swing both arms to the left. In order to reach this position you should now have twisted through the upper part of your body so that your right shoulder is leading slightly; then swing both arms to the right, wrapping your left arm around your waist. Now your left shoulder is, or should be, leading as your right shoulder is back, still with the right forearm fairly close to the shaft. Do not let your right elbow sneak forward! Immediately start walking or running while moving your crosse from left to right and back again. Should you experience difficulty, and you might, try stepping on the left foot as you cradle to the left, and then on the right foot as you cradle to the right. Another way to try to develop the rhythm is to skip.

The arm action in running is of course a forward-backward movement, and although the rhythm will remain the same, the motion of the left arm will be different because of the shoulder action. The left arm will remain at least at a right angle in order to keep the left hand waist high, and as you begin to move with more ease, speed and confidence, the left hand might well swing slightly upward. If the arm is at a right angle, with the elbow close to the side but not attached, the arm should swing outward, so that as you look down you can see the inside of your forearm. As you cradle to the right, the forearm will wrap around your middle bringing your hand above your right hip. This action of the left arm is like a gate opening and closing. As you run, check occasionally upon the movement of this arm. Train it as soon as you can.

Added to this swing of the arms is the action of both wrists which completes the movement of wrapping the crosse around the ball. As you hold your crosse up in front of you, the face or pocket is toward you. As you swing to the left, extend your left wrist and flex and rotate inward your right wrist so that the pocket of the crosse is facing forward (open). Swinging back to the right, the wrists reverse their action so that the pocket of the crosse is once again forward. In its complete action the path of the crosse is semi-circular, the pocket of the crosse open at either end of the cradling action. The smoothness of this semi-circular action, keeping the crosse always around the ball, keeps the ball in the crosse. Should you have difficulty, just watch your crosse as it moves to see at what point you shake the ball out. Most likely you are not completing the wrist action as the arms swing. Also continue to check your grip! (Figure 4 and 5)

Figure 5—Cradling Right

Figure 6—Cradling High

BASIC TECHNIQUES

Undoubtedly, as you begin, the ball will be sitting on the bridge of your crosse, but when you learn to relax through your shoulders and grip your crosse with only enough firmness to turn it, the ball will eventually be carried half way up the pocket. Try to feel the weight of the ball in your crosse. This should make you relax more.

Sometimes try cradling with just the bottom arm, then with just the top arm. Then with both arms cradle on the left, which means that as you run your right shoulder will lead, your arms now moving in a similar plane but with a smaller action. Then cradle on the right side with your left shoulder leading. Try cradling up high, top arm almost at full stretch. At this point it will perhaps seem illogical to cradle on the left and on the right, but the purpose is more than just an exercise. As you run rapidly, the challenge of keeping the ball in your crosse increases, and it should, with practice, increase flexibility through the upper part of your body and shoulders. More importantly, the ability to cradle on either side, moving your crosse from side to side with great assurance and speed, will prepare you for dodging an opponent, a skill that will come later but remarkably quickly if you have mastered cradling. (Figure 6)

Mentioned earlier was the problem of the elbow moving backward in the cradling, instead of keeping the elbow toward your side with the forearm swinging outward. As a check on yourself, stand with your back against a wall and cradle. As you swing to the left, your left hand should touch the wall before your elbow. Similarly as you swing to the right, the knuckles of the bottom hand should touch the wall on that side of you. A partner can hold her crosse just above your waist at the back and you can use this as the barrier. Also, if you cradle while running away from her, she *should* see your arm swinging outward each time you swing to the side of the bottom arm. As you run back toward her, she should be able to see the inside of that forearm with each swing.

Stand directly opposite and close to a partner, each in a good forward stride position. Practice cradling on one side, and then suddenly change to the other side. As you change from one side to the other, keep the head of your crosse well back over your head, your top hand forehead height

Figure 7—Cradling Facing Partner

or above. In this way you will avoid your partner's crosse. The quickness of the change from side to side plus practice in avoiding contact with your partner's crosse will add not only flexibility to the upper part of your body, but will make the art of dodging that much easier. It is important as you move from side to side to remember to watch your partner and not let your head turn to the side you are cradling on. The latter is a natural tendency which must be avoided. The ability to look left, right or forward despite the side you are cradling on is a *must* when you begin to play. (Figure 7)

Perhaps as you run doing this basic movement you will feel that you are wiggling all over and you may feel terribly awkward. Don't be troubled as you are not the first one to feel so, nor will you be the last. As you become more and more acquainted with your crosse, the freedom of the movement will gradually become a part of you. Keep a constant check on your grip.

PICKING UP A STATIONARY BALL. Though lacrosse is an aerial game, you have no doubt already experienced dropping the ball to the ground. Only the goalkeeper may touch the ball with her hands. How can you get the ball into your crosse efficiently, surely, and on your initial effort when you are madly chased by an opponent who is intent upon getting it first? The most exhausting part of the whole game is to be repeatedly unsuccess-

Figure 8—Picking Up (Stationary) Ball

Stand with your back against a wall. Can you cradle to the left so that your left hand touches before the elbow? Can you swing to the right so that the knuckles of the bottom hand touch the wall on your right?

Evaluation Questions

ful when endeavouring to pick up the ball. The ensuing scramble breaks the flow of the game; it is annoying and frustrating to all players.

As you approach the ball, place your right foot directly beside it. With your knees bent, right shoulder leading, head down so that you may see the ball, and the butt end of your crosse almost touching the ground, scoop up the ball by making a slight arc-like movement. As it comes into your crosse begin to cradle immediately, probably first to your left as your body is slightly turned in this direction. As you cradle, get your crosse and your

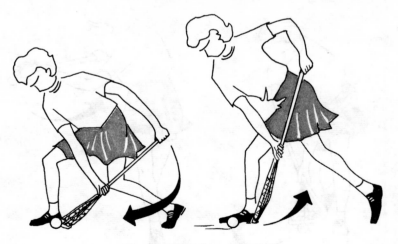

Figure 9—Picking Up Ball

A. Stationary Ball   B. Ball moving towards player
                                   pp. 24 and 25

body into an upright position as soon as possible. Pick up the ball on the side of your bottom hand, never with the crosse directly in front of you, for safety and efficiency. The grip on your crosse is still the same and you should notice how perfect the position of both hands is for executing this particular skill. (Figure 8)

If the ball bobbles and bounces around in your crosse as you pick it up, this may result from tension in your grip, failure to "feel" the ball in your crosse and lack of instant cradling. If your crosse gets under the ball all right, but hits the bridge and comes back out again, you are perhaps jabbing at the ball, moving the crosse straight under it, rather than using a slight arc-like movement. *Do not flick the ball into the air* and then try to catch it. Not only is this poor technique, possibly laziness in "getting down to it," but flicking the ball can become dangerous and therefore a *foul*. Never stop to pick up the ball as you would a tennis ball, as this also is poor technique.

Start immediately picking up a stationary ball by running and spacing your approach so that the right foot is *opposite or beside* the ball. Perfection of this skill is related to your future enjoyment of the game. It cannot be overpracticed! Have your partner stand and hold her crosse out to the side at shoulder height. Place a ball on the ground under it. Run and pick up the ball keeping low enough to avoid your partner's crosse. Can you do it if she holds her crosse a little lower?

Should the ball be running *away from you* along the ground, you must run faster and make your low swoop under the ball that much quicker. What must now be in your mind is the question of a ball coming *toward* you along the ground. As the principle for this situation is similar to catching the ball in the air, it will be discussed later in this chapter.

CATCHING. Perhaps it seems strange to approach this technique when you have yet to learn to throw! However, you can gain great confidence in the movement of your crosse by tossing the ball to yourself, or by having a partner toss it to you by hand. Catching has often been described as "wrapping the crosse around the ball" or "surrounding the ball with the crosse." Two principles in catching are self-evident: there must be a "give" and the implement must be prepared to receive the ball. Consider the pocket of the crosse as the palm of your hand. It must always be behind the path of the ball. To say the ball is caught at one end of the cradling motion or the other might not make sense at this point. In cradling, your crosse faces forward, then toward you, then opens again as it completes its circular action. Therefore if a ball is coming toward you on the right, as it enters the crosse, the crosse will cradle left and then continue its motion. Similarly, if the ball is on your left, give slightly as you cradle back to the right. Once again, your grip is important and it is still the same. *Always reach for the ball with your top hand.* The position of your right hand will seem strange because of the way it is turned to catch the ball on your right. (Figure 10 and 11)

However, the hand is ready in this position to start the cradling action as the ball enters the crosse. The position or grip of the right hand is quite perfect for catching on the left, ready to begin the movement of the crosse back to the right. The left hand is always ready with its firm grip to begin its share of the cradling. If the right arm is extended out to reach for the ball, the butt end of the crosse is therefore pointing more toward the body. The expression "extending the top arm" must not be construed to imply tension. If the arm is stiff there can be no "give" as you "gather in" the ball.

While running, toss the ball out of your crosse to yourself at various heights and distances. Toss it so that you will get equal catching practice both on the left and right sides. Practice catching at various levels and always on the move. Reach up or out, depending upon where the ball is, with your top hand, making certain your crosse is ready to receive the ball. As the ball enters, "give" slightly as you begin to cradle. Collect the ball into your crosse as soon as you can, at your greatest height or reach. By doing this you may well out-reach your opponent in a game. Try to get a good twist through your waist and shoulders as you catch and cradle the ball, for in the game you will want to swing your crosse away from your opponent who will most likely be trying to catch the same pass.

Figure 10—Catching

In the game you will "ask for the ball," indicating your readiness to receive it by pointing your crosse into the space to which you are moving. As your partner tosses the ball to you either by hand or with her crosse, *it is most important that you show where you want the ball* by showing the direction with your crosse and by moving your feet. You will never be free enough in a game to stand still as you receive a pass. Rather, you will be running at top speed trying to lose your opponent. Practice this and as you do so, moving both to the left and the right, your partner will be learning to throw the ball into a space with the correct timing and force so that the ball and crosse meet without the pace being broken. To simplify this practice, have your partner just toss the ball to you as you run around her counterclockwise, and later clockwise. Return each toss to her the best way you can. Eventually you will want to practice asking for a pass as you run not just left or right, but sometimes diagonally forward or diagonally backward left and right, and toward the player with the ball.

Should you have a lacrosse ball or a tennis ball and wall nearby, you can have great practice by yourself.

THE SHOULDER PASS. This particular pass is the most often used. Why? As you have cradled, you perhaps have noticed that your crosse moves perpendicular to the ground and in line with your body. Every

Figure 11—Catching

Figure 12—Shoulder Pass

cradling action brings your crosse to your right, your throwing side; your right shoulder and arm are almost in a perfect throwing position. You can pass quickly and at a moment's notice—so necessary in this game. There are several fundamental points which must be fully understood, practiced and remembered. Checking these points constantly will hasten your learning.

First of all, the shoulder pass is a lever pass and the amount of leverage used determines the distance of the throw. Other factors determine the direction and the intent—meaning the path of the ball: direct or a looping path, or even a downward path as used so often in shooting.

1. To prepare for a throw, bring your crosse over to your right side close to you, with your left hand to your right hip or just above. This will bring your left shoulder forward and your right shoulder back.

2. *Then lift the butt end of your crosse in the direction you wish the pass to go. This is most important as it determines the direction.* At this juncture the grip of your right hand will seem awkward and odd and completely useless for throwing, so slip your hand *just a little* behind, but not directly behind, the crosse in order that the wrist can relax backwards. (If you were throwing a ball with your hand this is how your wrist would be.)

3. As you extend your right arm upward, at the same time pull the butt end of the crosse into your right arm pit. This is your lever action— this sumultaneous "give and take" between the left and right hands and arms, the left giving the power and the direction, and the right the control. From the beginning see that your right arm finishes straight and the left hand up under the right arm. The flicking action or follow-through of the right wrist gives the finishing touch.

The three actions of this pass must of course be done while running and even though your feet are going forward you must be able to pass to the left, straight ahead or to the right. The three actions have no short cut but eventually, as you become more skillful in their execution and therefore familiar with the feel of the total movement, you will be less conscious of them as three actions.

If you drop the ball in the process of throwing, there may be several reasons: (1) In your eagerness to throw it is possible that you missed the first action of bringing your entire crosse to the right; probably instead, as you brought your right shoulder back, you lifted the butt end straight away which produced a flinging, slinging action and out went the ball. Or (2) perhaps as you came over to the right you failed to complete the cradling action which is necessary to keep your crosse behind or under the ball at this point. Or (3) while preparing to throw you might have held the butt end of the crosse up and the ball rolled out of the back. Once the butt end is lifted in preparation, this action must be rapidly followed by the pull back to the arm pit. This will then start the ball rolling up and out of the crosse in the desired direction. (Figure 12)

In the beginning the whole action will be done with the movement of the right hand and arm fairly close to your head. As your confidence increases this same lever pass can be done at varying levels.

Take a partner and run beside one another five to ten yards apart, throwing to one another and catching. You will notice that the one on the left must get more twist in the upper part of her body as she throws to the right. Change places on your return trip. If you are the receiver, don't forget to point with your crosse where you wish to receive the ball. If you are the thrower, try to place the ball right in your partner's crosse. As you catch the pass, see how quickly you can control the ball with your cradling in order to pass again as soon as possible. Don't overindulge yourself with time. Should you drop the ball, run, pick it up and carry on. This will help to build your endurance. Another practice is to run in a circle counterclockwise with your partner, throwing and catching in turn.

THE PIVOT TURN. When catching was discussed it was suggested that you should run in various directions asking for the pass. In a game you often receive the ball with your back toward the goal you are attacking. As everyone is coached to run directly toward the goal when in possession of the ball (though always watching for someone to whom to pass) it is impor-

Can you successfully mirror your partner's forward and sideward movements and footwork in this practice?

Evaluation Questions
PRACTICING BODY CHECKING

tant to be able to turn immediately—not only to try to evade your opponent but also to get moving in the proper direction.

To turn to the left is a very simple maneuver yet this must not imply that the pivot to the right is difficult; it is just different. The basic move-

Figure 13—Pivot Turn

Diagram B:

PRACTICING
BODY CHECKING

ment with your shoulders and your crosse is exactly the same as your cradling from left to right, and the same as the swing of your crosse from left to right as you prepare for the shoulder pass. As stated previously, it is this connecting link between one technique and another that makes this game unique in its simplicity and duplication of movement.

Stand in a forward stride position with the left foot ahead. Take your crosse well to your left with a good twist of your shoulders. Next bring your crosse over to the right, left hand touching your right hip or just above, and the right hand should brush close to your head. The swing from left to right must be quick in order to keep the crosse under or behind the ball. Then pivot on the balls of your feet to your right, facing the opposite direction—and there is your crosse ready to start its cradling movement to the left as you begin to run. Each time you practice, run, stop with left foot forward and pull your crosse to the left at the same time. Then swing your crosse to your right, *followed* by the pivot on your toes, and as soon as you are facing in the opposite direction start to cradle and run immediately. Eventually, the swing of the crosse over to the right and the pivot will be done simultaneously, not in two separate parts as explained above. (Figure 13)

Are you dropping the ball and if so at what point? Check again the action of your wrists and arms. Are you forgetting to keep the crosse behind or under the ball with quick wrist action as you move from left to right? If so, you will have flung the ball out.

For a practice, stand about ten yards away from a partner. Place the ball on the ground halfway between your positions. One of you *run* forward, pick up the ball, controlling both it and yourself in time to do a pivot turn before your partner is reached. Return to where you started, do another pivot turn and then replace the ball on the ground so that your partner may take her turn. As soon as possible, increase the speed of picking up and turning. Have your partner hold her crosse up high and slanted slightly forward. Do your pivot turn *under* her crosse, avoiding her crosse with yours.

Figure 14—Body Checking

BODY CHECKING. The term sounds ominous but it is not. Earlier it was mentioned that there is no personal contact in this game. Body checking is placing oneself between the player with the ball and the goal she is attacking, moving always with her. This particular skill is vitally important and must be practiced often. There is a tremendous challenge in its proper execution and one is rewarded with a feeling of satisfaction when it is successfully accomplished during a game. Your teammates' chances of success will be much enhanced if you body-check well, and your opponents will experience frustration. The successful body-checker may be thought of as a shadow. Did you ever try to elude your shadow when you were young, darting hither and thither and with a sudden burst of speed try to evade it? The skillful body-checker sticks as closely as a shadow. Fortunately in a game, through feinting and dodging it is sometimes possible to escape this shadow, otherwise the game would come to a standstill.

Why body check? A player with the ball must head straight for the goal at top speed. Can you picture your opponent moving toward you at top speed with the ability to twist and dodge by you? Should you not be able to body check, your opponent will be well on her way and your team will be minus a player—you—left behind! A good body-checker, by her own quick movement, is able to force her opponent from her direct path of attack, slow her down by constantly moving with her thus forcing her to pass. These are your aims. However, to reach this standard takes determination and effort.

You must be able to run backward and sideways at great speed with quick steps, balanced over the balls of your feet, so that you can change direction easily as your opponent with the ball tries to dodge past you. Running backward is no easy task as one tends to become over-balanced. One way to practice without your crosses is to have a partner who faces you arms length away. Place your hands on one another's shoulders. Your partner will begin to move forward and sideways changing her direction

20

at will. Your task is to stay with her. [As she moves forward, swerving her hips and feet from side to side, you match her movements attempting to stay always with her.] Mirror her path with your body and footwork, striving to keep your steps small and quick, with sufficient balance to change direction as dictated by the person initiating the movement. As it is impossible to run as fast backward as your opponent can run forward, it will be necessary for you to twist in such a way that your hips and feet move in the same direction as your partner. This practice can be great fun and a challenge, and should be practiced often. (Diagram B)

Now with your crosse. You have practiced cradling on the left and right and switching quickly from side to side. This was the beginning of dodging. You, as the body checker, must try to follow the path of your opponent's cradling movements with your crosse. It is not necessary for *you* to cradle as you don't have the ball. Your grip must be firm on your crosse, but *your arms must not be stiff or tense.* Have your partner stand at least five yards away and start toward you. You must immediately start to move backward, your crosse well-balanced in front of you. The person with the ball will wait until she gets quite close to you before attempting to get by you with either a quick twist and a burst of speed or by feinting from side to side trying to get you off-balance. As you match her footwork and speed, follow her crosse as it moves with your crosse, always being conscious that you must never endanger her face and head or any part of her body. Should she finally break by you, immediately follow by running beside her keeping your crosse always in line with hers, but you may not touch her or hold your crosse against her. As she becomes more confident, she might well suddenly change her direction to the other side, having succeeded in pulling you in one direction. You must be ready for this, skillful and balanced enough to match her changes of direction. Never give up. (Figure 14)

POINTS TO REMEMBER. Do not wait until your opponent is almost upon you before you start moving backward in her path. Remember she is coming at top speed and you will be easily passed. You should move immediately when you see her with the ball; your very presence between her and her goal will have an effect. You, as the body-checker, must be what would be described on the roads as a hazardous driver, the person who always speeds up and shifts lanes slightly just as you are trying to pass.

Your shadow-like presence, your crosse opposite your opponent's crosse, your determination and "stick-to-it-iveness" will have a daunting effect on your opponent. You will slow her down, force her wide of her path, or force her to pass, and this pass should be intercepted by one of your teammates. If possible, you must try to dislodge the ball from your opponent's crosse or block the pass. *Remember—crosse checking comes after or with body checking—not before it or instead of it.*

CROSSE CHECKING. This is an addition to and not a substitute for body-checking. Your purpose in crosse checking is to dislodge the ball from your opponent's crosse.

Your hands remain in the same position as for all other techniques. Should your top hand slip down the shaft in order to get greater reach, the leverage of the action changes and you will find that your control of the movement of the crosse is lessened. Crosse checking *poorly done* causes roughness. Properly done, it is a very fair means of dislodging the ball. The action, mainly done with the wrists, is one of short, sharp, quick taps of your crosse down or up on your opponent's crosse. Use the wood or backbone of the crosse for the contact. Your aim is to dislodge the ball so that it will drop to the ground or even pop into the air so that you can catch it. This latter action is rather advanced and can only be accomplished by tapping upward on your opponent's crosse. It may well be that in the beginning stages you will be allowed only to tap downward, until your footwork and balance in body checking allow you to move with the speed and control necessary for checking upward without endangering your opponent in *any way*. The previous sentence should not be construed to imply that balance and control are not necessary for *all* crosse checking, whether up or down. When crosse checking and trying to intercept a shoulder pass, it is well to *aim about a foot higher* than you think the ball will leave your opponent's crosse. This will not only prevent knocked knuckles but will also prove more effective.

Should your opponent be running alongside you with her crosse away from you, you are not allowed to reach your crosse over her head or across her body in order to impede her progress—you may not endanger her in any way. Should your opponent pass you and you are quickly dashing after her, you may not reach over her shoulder to try to check her crosse which undoubtedly is being cradled in front of her. Should she, of course, bring her crosse back in preparation for a pass, or foolishly carry her crosse on the side, then it may be possible for you to tap your crosse sharply against hers and dislodge the ball.

Never stand still and just attempt to reach out and crosse-check as an opponent rushes by, and never attempt checking if you are off-balance. In all games, the person is of paramount importance, so consideration, care and control must be exercised—sometimes these must supercede your determination to win.

DODGING. How to get by an opponent who is determined to stay between you and your goal no matter which way you move, is what we must deal with next. If possible, always pass the ball as it can arrive sooner than you can, but make sure that it is sent to someone in a better position than you are. *A good pass is always better than a dodge!*

If you have the ball, move toward your goal with great speed. If the man-to-man marking is successful, you will always have an opponent near ready to body check and crosse check you.

The ability to cradle on your left and your right with tremendous twisting in the upper part of your body so that your body is between your crosse and your opponent, plus speed of foot for swerving and feinting left and right to throw your opponent momentarily off balance, are the qualities to strive for in executing the dodge.

Keeping your crosse moving in the same axis as your body and close to you, and keeping it as close to your head as possible as you switch from side to side, are important. Your head must be up, not ducked as you try to get past, for you must be able to watch your opponent's crosse *and* also look for someone to whom to pass. (Figures 15 and 16)

Remember, you are the one running forward, certainly an easier position to be in. You can see the goal you are attacking, and your teammates who should be getting free to receive a pass from you. Certainly you have an advantage over your opponent if you are wise enough, skillful enough and fast enough to use it. *Once you get by your opponent* remember to cradle in front of you and not let your crosse drop down to the side. Your opponent should and will be in hot pursuit, trying to check your crosse. However, she is *not allowed by rules, or by sanity* to reach over your shoulder with her crosse to try to check your crosse.

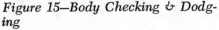

Figure 15—Body Checking & Dodging

Figure 16—Dodging

Can you and your partner successfully complete ten underarm passes
to each other while running in a
small circle?

Evaluation Questions

PRACTICING THE
UNDERARM PASS

Do not start your dodge too far away from your opponent as this will make it easier for her to move into your path. Rather, run straight on and just before you get to her, begin to swerve and try to pass her. Do not turn your back on her, (i.e., turning all the way around,) as you are then oblivious of a teammate moving to help; your sense of direction and your forward movement will be lost, and you will be completely at the mercy of your opponent.

As a beginner you perhaps feel safer and more secure turning your back on your opponent as you decide which side to go by, because you are bothered by her constant presence and her ever present crosse shadowing yours. *Make yourself face forward* and keep your shoulders and feet and hips moving, as your eyes observe and as you determine the next move.

Constant practice of dodging against an opponent will be time well spent. The ability to look both left and right as well as straight ahead as you twist from side to side is most important as you make your decision whether to go on or to pass to a teammate.

There will be many occasions when there will be only one opponent between you and the goal you are attacking. The ability to dodge successfully may determine whether or not you will have the chance to shoot a goal.

THE LOW CATCH OR THE BALL COMING TOWARD YOU ON THE GROUND. In catching, as previously described, the crosse was in an upright position, the top hand reaching out for the ball. The crosse must be behind the flight of the ball, so for a low catch (although the top or right hand still reaches out) the left hand will be uppermost or, to put it briefly, the crosse will be inverted. In catching any ball chest height or above with your hand, your fingers point upward; if below the waist the fingers point downward. If you think of the pocket of the crosse as similar to the palm of your hand, the position of your crosse should be self-evident.

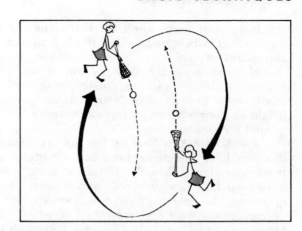

Diagram C:

PRACTICING THE UNDERARM PASS

Let us think about the ball coming toward you along the ground. You have learned to pick up a stationary ball on the ground by placing your right foot beside the ball and then picking it up on the side of your bottom or left hand. Your head was over the ball, your right shoulder leading. These four points are equally applicable for this new skill! For the stationary ball or the one rolling away from you, the action of the crosse was a low arc moving under the ball, and at one moment the left hand almost touched the ground. Should you put the crosse in this position for a ball coming *toward* you at any speed, one of two things would happen: the ball would either come into your crosse and go right on over it, or it would hit the bridge of your crosse and bounce out. The greater the speed of the ball the *more perpendicular* your crosse must be. As you run toward the ball, your crosse must be ready to receive it beside your right foot. As the ball enters you must give backward with your crosse in order to absorb the impact, and you must start your cradling action as your feet continue to move forward. You will be greatly assisted in the cradling and the giving if your right shoulder points downward toward the ball. Should you make the mistake of bringing your crosse forward as the ball enters the crosse, you will certainly "bat" the ball out. The "give" followed by the cradling, an almost simultaneous action, is the same as in every catch—the amount of give depending upon your speed and the speed of the ball. Absorption of impact is important. (Figure 9b)

When doing this inverted or low catch, bring your crosse up and into your forward cradle as soon as possible, not only to protect your crosse from being checked but also to be prepared for the next move.

Practicing this particular skill is great fun and gives one a feeling of swooping and swerving. The "give" through the body, the twist of the shoulders, the gathering in of the ball, make for such a complete feeling of movement.

25

Have your partner roll the ball along the ground to you quite hard. Approach it with speed, gather the ball in, control it, and then pivot turn and return to your place. Now do the same for your partner. Your partner should throw bouncing shots to you as well. Should you have difficulty getting the feeling of your crosse giving backward and into a cradle in this inverted position, have your partner toss the ball to you around knee height on your left side. A low catch and a ball moving toward you on the ground are similar.

THE UNDER-ARM PASS OR THE SHOVEL PASS. By now you have realized that you have sometimes been at a disadvantage because you can throw from your right side only. If this were to remain true it would be like having no backhand in tennis and what a disadvantage that is! With an opponent who hovers around you, moves with you, hampers the movement of your crosse with her crosse (all of which she is supposed to do), you of course must be able to pass to a teammate from either side.

As you bring your crosse to your left, emphasize the twist of your shoulders even more—very similar to the movement of dodging an opponent on your right. Actually it is this twist, almost turning your back on your opponent, which makes this pass difficult to check because it is protected somewhat by your body. The head of your crosse, having been brought well behind you, now drops down as the left hand comes high, the right hand having guided the head of the crosse in a C shape. Momentarily the crosse will be perpendicular to the ground in the inverted position but the ball will not fall or roll out if the movement is continuous. The height of the right hand at the end of the throw will determine the height

Figure 17—Underarm Pass

of the throw, and the amount of leverage and action will determine the distance. Both arms move in a parallel action. Do not let the right arm be stiff on the release of the pass—the ball will shoot out rather than be controlled. When this pass is used as a shot for goal, then this is a different matter. (Figure 17)

It is important to "feel" the ball in your crosse during this throw. At first you might well drop the ball as you go through the motions. Don't be surprised or upset. Most likely you have made the action too slow and so the ball rolled out as you inverted the crosse. Avoid a backward forward action of the crosse parallel to the ground, propelling the ball straight from the bridge of the crosse.

The shovel pass can travel from quite a short to quite a long way and it can be most useful. However, it must not be done in preference to the shoulder pass, should you have a choice at the moment of throwing, because the shoulder pass can be executed more quickly as it "comes out" of your cradling action. To prepare for an under-arm pass takes slightly longer and is therefore more easily followed by your opponent's crosse.

To practice this pass, you and your partner walk and then *run* in a small circle clockwise, passing the ball back and forth to one another. *Be sure* to look toward the person to whom you are passing and do not let your head turn to the left as you cradle to the left in preparation for this pass. *Guessing* where your partner or teammate is, rather than *looking* toward her, is a common mistake. You naturally want to follow the motion of your crosse to see if you still have the ball, but try to feel it in your crosse; this suggestion will also help you to develop smoothness of action in your arms, shoulders, etc. You will notice as you practice in this formation that you are turned so that the upper part of your back is toward the person to whom you are throwing.

Also practice running beside your partner. The person on the right will shoulder pass to you and you, in turn, will throw back to her using the under-arm pass.

GOAL SHOOTING. Any hard shot at goal must be low. To score a goal by terrororizing the goalkeeper because it is high and hard is hardly the kind of goal you would be pleased to claim. You will already have learned about the circle around the goal called the *crease*, but only when you begin to practice shooting will the real meaning of the crease become evident. It is special protection for the goalkeeper and it is a challenge to you as the shooter. Were there no protective space, the goalkeeper's task would be impossible. As it is, she is still at your mercy in many ways.

The rules of the crease for the attack are clear, concise and fair. Very simply, no player may have her crosse over the crease before, during or after the shot. It is the "after" that players seem to be the most careless about. When running toward the crease at great speed, or swerving around it, it is very possible that the momentum used in shooting can carry either your crosse or your body or both over the crease after the release. If this

Can you and your partners keep the ball going for three rounds with a shoulder pass from 1 to 2, an underarm pass from 2 to 3, and an underarm shot along the ground from 3 to 1?

Evaluation Questions

PRACTICING
TWO PASSES

happens, even if the ball enters the goal, it is disallowed. Here, as in every other part of the game, *space awareness is vitally important.*

THE OVER-ARM BOUNCING SHOT. The execution of this shot is a continuation of the shoulder pass. There the head of the crosse indicated the height and direction of the pass and the right arm was fully extended upward at the end of the pass, the right wrist having produced the final control necessary for accuracy. The left hand finished up under the right arm. To produce a fast and downward path to the ball, the head of the crosse is brought sharply downward, the left hand ending up on the outside of the right shoulder. The follow-through of the whole body is a strong one. Remember that this action is done while running at top speed. The

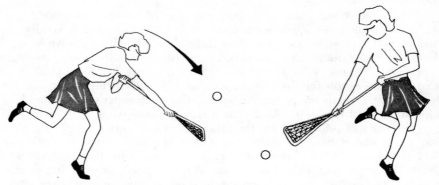

Figure 18—Overarm Bouncing Shot   Figure 19—Underarm Shot for Goal

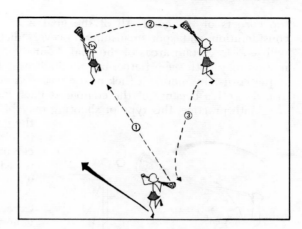

Diagram D:

PRACTICING
TWO PASSES

shooter's objective is to have the ball hit the ground just inside the crease and bounce into the unprotected corner of the goal. (Figure 18)

You must have a clear space in front of the goal before you attempt this shot and you must not shoot the ball into the midst of the defense. It is a shot that can be done some distance from the goal and is a most useful one for the attack wings, or any other player for that matter who has broken free, when there is a clear space between her and the goal.

If done while running at top speed with correct arm and wrist action and a forceful follow-through, this shot can travel at great speed and either bounce low and into the goal, or slither along the ground with a devastating spin.

THE UNDER-ARM SHOT. This is a wonderfully deceptive shot that travels along the ground or close to it and can be done with greater power when you are almost "back to" the goal. As in the under-arm pass, the body twists toward the left or the side of your bottom hand. The follow-through of the head of your crosse is low, pointing toward the ground, right arm straight. It is terribly important to release the ball low so it will not rise upward toward the goalkeeper or any other player. (Figure 19)

This shot is most useful in two particular situations: (1) You are being well body checked by an opponent, making an overarm shot impossible, and so with a quick dodge to the left you place your body between your opponent and your crosse and shoot; (2) You have cut into a space, moving across in front of the goal which is on your right, and receiving a pass, you immediately shoot. You can execute this shot when you are quite well past the goal, provided, you can see it (over your right shoulder) well enough to aim.

HIGH OVER-ARM SHOOTING. The two previous shots have two definite points in common. They are hard and they are low. Now what about the

29

top corners of the goal? All of the goal is there to be used! Sensitivity, consideration and sportsmanship, however, dictate the kind of shot you will send to certain areas of the goal. Your expression and your attitude of motion may both seem fierce, but the ball must be placed softly into either upper corner by merely a flick of the wrists as you pop it in. Safe, yes! and also deceptive because of the change of pace in the flight of the ball.

With practice, this type of shooting may be done as you move toward the goal or as you move across it in either direction. Practice receiving a high catch and follow it with a quick flick—always while moving. (Figure 20)

In most sports books you expect to find a chapter on advanced techniques. All skills described in this chapter are essential to playing lacrosse, but, strangely enough, there are no more! What leads to success and therefore pleasure, is perfecting these techniques, developing the ability to perform them with smoothness and speed under all circumstances, and then using them well in combination with your teammates.

Figure 20—High Corners Shot

3

Aspects of the Game

In order to participate fully, it is important for you to know more about certain aspects of lacrosse. Before considering attack and defense play, it is necessary to pull together certain terms and concepts you have already met: 'draw,' 'throw-on,' 'free position;' dodging, man-to-man marking and body-checking; words such as initiative, space awareness, speed, balance, observation and control.

Let us begin with the skills which are the essence of the game. How does a player get free to receive a pass when being marked closely, or if a player is free to run anywhere to receive a pass, how does the defending player deal with such a situation? The first part of the question involves "cutting for a pass" or "making a dodge into a space to receive a pass." The second part requires *marking*. As marking makes the cutting or dodging necessary, it seems wise to begin with the cause. Marking requires a combination of determination, tenacity, nimble and neat footwork, the ability to change direction quickly to match your opponent's moves as she attempts to get free, and also the courage, decision and speed necessary for possible interception.

If you have played basketball or hockey, you will remember that in the beginning you were told who your opponent was and that you were directly responsible for causing her to lose effectiveness. This could be accomplished by intercepting the ball before she received it, or by either trying to rob her of the ball or forcing her to pass. In lacrosse, man-to-man marking is the fundamental method of defense from the beginning stages through international play. This is one of the things that makes the game unique; the challenge to each individual makes the spacing of the attack possible and should prohibit crowding in front of the goal. Crowding results in dangerous play and frustration.

You will no doubt immediately question the possibility of a player with the ball suddenly being able to evade her opponent and break free or clear. Later under defense play, you will learn about an interchange which will deal with this question.

To mark properly, you should feel almost "stuck" to your opponent, yet without actual contact. With one foot slightly in front and one foot slightly behind her, your crosse in the direction of hers, you are ready to intercept, if possible, any pass to her. Your opponent will move in various directions trying to lose you. She might feint one way and then dart another to throw you off her trail. She will always ask for the ball (indicate with her crosse) on her free side, or to put it another way, away from your crosse. It should occur to you immediately, that you should not let your opponent get goal-side of you, free to catch or to shoot. Forcing her by your positioning always away from the center spaces will make it more difficult for her or her teammates to score. (Figures 21 and 22)

By staying close to your opponent and watching both her and the player with the ball, it will be possible with speed and determination to intercept a pass. However, should your opponent outwit you for a moment and you realize that to intercept the pass is impossible, you must immediately drop goal-side of her into the path she must take in order to run straight for goal, and begin to body check and crosse check. The one foot in front and the one behind gives you the correct balance to initiate a burst of speed forward to intercept, and the step behind should make you ready to body check. As your opponent becomes a better player, escaping you long enough to receive the ball, she will quickly pivot to catch you

Figure 21—Cutting and Marking to the right

Figure 22—Cutting and Marking to the left

off balance as she heads for the goal. Close marking is frustrating and difficult to play against; if you are several yards from your opponent she will be *extremely grateful* to you.

As you read the foregoing paragraphs did you feel frustrated or challenged? Perhaps a bit of both, but, it is hoped that challenge was the stronger reaction.

CUTTING OR GETTING FREE FOR A PASS. You now are the one who will try to evade your opponent, if only long enough to receive a pass. Is it easier to initiate a move or to follow one? Your intention, your idea, your path of movement will begin in your mind and your opponent must try to interpret your plan. Her reaction will take time, though the more skilled she becomes the faster that reaction will be. As she becomes better at her job, you may be but one stride ahead of her. However, that one stride is sufficient if the pass made to you is accurate and into the space into which you are moving. You must indicate where you want the ball by extending your crosse in that direction and then move at top speed to that spot so you will be ready, should you be, in the opinion of the player with the ball, the person in the best position to receive it.

Sometimes you will be able to get free with one sudden quick movement. At other times you must feint in several different ways and directions to throw your opponent off balance. It seems to be human nature to drop behind an opponent, hopefully expecting that a pass can reach you. During a game this possibility might well present itself and if so, by all means try it. However, a good defense player is also determined that you shall not get between her and the goal she is defending! Always remember that your teammate with the ball, harassed by an opponent who is body checking and attempting to crosse check as well, will find it difficult to pass to you if it is neceesary to pass both over her own opponent and over yours.

Lacrosse is really a game of "Keep Away," an unbroken series of passes from teammate to teammate until the player with the ball is in a position to shoot. To make this possible, the players must move to evade their opponents, most profitably directly left or right, diagonally forward left or right, diagonally backward left or right, or straight toward the player with the ball.

When indicating the direction you expect to move, it is important to ask for the ball on your "free" side: not toward your opponent but away from her. Your crosse must be away from hers.

When to begin your "cut," or movement to get free, is of vital importance. If you make your intention known too soon (before your teammate is prepared to pass the ball), when the pass finally comes your opponent may intercept it. When would your teammate *not* be ready to pass? (1) Certainly when she has received a pass with her back toward you. Wait until she turns. (2) When she is picking the ball up off the ground. (3) When she is just about to receive the ball herself. She must have time to

If the player on the right plays with the left hand up, how would her body position change in relation to her opponent?

Evaluation Questions

THE DRAW

catch it, control it, have a brief opportunity to observe your movement and the moves of her other teammates before deciding which one is in the best position to receive the next pass.

It is not to be assumed that you are standing still during these three situations! Constant moving, though not at great speed, will keep your opponent occupied and her attention divided between the player with the ball and you. Your moving about will worry her for she will not know where you eventually intend to cut, and also you will be making greater spaces into which to move. The correct timing of the act and the accuracy of the passing are of course *the game.*

The Rules dictate how a game is started and how it is restarted after a goal is scored, after a foul has occurred and after a ball has gone out of bounds or an accident has happened.

In lacrosse, the words 'draw,' 'free position' and 'throw-on' are the directions used by both teacher and umpire and the correct performance of the skills is important in determining whether an advantage is gained or lost. Most team games are started and stopped with a whistle. However, in lacrosse, play is always started or resumed with the words, "Ready-draw," or "Ready-play." The "Ready" is to prepare *all* players, not only those directly involved, and the "draw" or "play" is the signal that all players may move. This in itself is strange and unique. In other games players are constantly moving to get into position before play can resume. Once the game is stopped in lacrosse, however, except after a goal has been scored, players may not move to reposition themselves before the game recommences. An umpire may ask a player or players to move in order to fulfill the rules of the game, but she will direct them to do so and will indicate where they are to go. This may happen at the time of the draw, when no one may be within five yards of the draw, or when a free position is awarded and no player may be within five yards of the player who is about

Diagram E:

THE DRAW

to have the free position. There are certain other occasions when players are directed to move but these will be made clear later in a more general rules discussion.

THE DRAW. This is how the game is started at the beginning of each half, after each goal is scored, when a double foul occurs, and at any other time when play has been stopped for some reason and no foul has occurred.

The draw to begin the game, and after each goal is scored, is referred to as the *center draw*. The following description will take the center draw as the example, merely because of the center line. (In all other draws the line is imaginary, and at right angles to the goal.) Having looked at a diagram of the field, you will have noticed a center circle with a line in the center. (Diagram 1.) All players other than the two opposing centers must be outside this circle until the draw is completed, that is to say, until the ball is up and away.

The two center players stand each with one foot touching the line and their crosses in front of them parallel to the line, and the wood of the crosses parallel to one another. Diagram E. The ball is placed between the backs of the crosses which means that the player's crosse is between the ball and the goal she is defending. It would seem easier to say that these players stand with their backs to the goal they are defending. However, should one of the players play with her *left hand up,* she will be facing the same direction as her opponent but her crosse will be properly placed between ball and goal.

Once the ball is properly placed, each player exerting enough pressure against her opponent's crosse to keep the ball from falling out, begins the necessary impetus when the command is given. The umpire will say "Ready-draw." The timing between these words must allow just the right time lapse to prevent too much preparation on the part of either player, thus giving neither too much advantage. Do not expect the words, "Ready-draw," to be said always with the same timing. The umpire will alter the timing

35

and will watch carefully between her words for any motion of the crosses which might give an unfair advantage to one or the other. At the final command, each player will, with a quick rotation of her wrists, try to capture the ball on her crosse, move her arms quickly upward and outward leading with her top hand out toward her left attack. The ball should go up and out one direction or the other. Both players must move their crosse in an upward action and the ball must at least rise above their heads. Should the ball go straight up or at least near the players taking the draw there is no rule that prevents them from trying to gain possession of it. The ball is "fair game" for either team as it moves upward and outward. Should the ball not go at least above the players' heads, the draw is repeated. As soon as the draw is complete, other players may enter the circle, Only two players should move for it and all others should pull away in order to create spaces for them and for the play which will follow. It is always easier and quicker to move toward a ball than to chase after it. This is why the centers should not chase in the direction the ball moves but allow the other players to come toward it. This helps to eliminate the danger of colliding.

All players should practice the draw, for any could be called upon to do it. The feel of your opponent's crosse aginst yours, the quick action of the wrists and the strong upward, outward action of the arms must be experienced over and over in order to realize the effort as well as the advantage that could be gained with its proper execution.

FREE POSITION. We have talked about the draw as a way to restart play after a double foul, but now consider the single foul. In this case, the player fouled against is awarded the ball where the foul occurred, unless it is within ten yards of the goal. All other players must be five yards away. On the word "play," the player with the ball *may run, pass* or *shoot.* What must be remembered is that once the word "play" is heard, any opponent may immediately move in to body check and/or crosse check. One could say the player has a rapid five yard decision to make, for her freedom of action is short lived.

THE THROW-IN OR THROW-ON. There are no boundaries on the lacrosse field. However, unless there are natural barriers which are in themselves limiting, or unless the umpire uses her discretion as to space, the game could go far afield, be pointless and exhausting. The term *Out of Bounds* might seem contradictory for it was stated that there are no boundaries. However, common sense dictates there must be some limits. The umpire's discretion is not needed while a player has the ball. It is the ball that goes far afield, or against a fence or under a tree or even among the spectators which calls for her attention. At the moment when the umpire decides to whistle, it is easy to determine whether if play were allowed to continue, one player would easily get to the ball first, or whether it would be an even race between the two opponents. Should it be the first of these two situations, at the sound of the whistle all players stand still and the one who is closest retrieves the ball as directed by the umpire. She brings it back over the path where it went out and as she returns to the field of play, the umpire says "play" and the game continues. This is not to be considered a 'free position.' The player is merely in possession of the ball which is what would have happened anyway had the game been allowed to continue. The umpire rightly saved the player or players from wasting unnecessary energy.

Figure 23—The Throw on

Should the two opponents be equally in hot pursuit, the game is restarted with a 'throw-on.' If they have an equal opportunity of retrieving the ball when the whistle blows, the umpire considers this equality. The two players stand side by side, the defending player on the goal side of her opponent, at a place indicated by the umpire, about one yard apart so as to avoid personal contact in the ensuing action. The umpire stands with her back to the center of the field, about ten yards from the players. She then says "ready" followed by the word "play." At this moment, she sends a short, high underhand toss toward and between the two contestants. The ability to accelerate and move in to receive the ball is put to the test. As you catch the ball, cradle away from your opponent for you can be easily crosse-checked by her. You must avoid touching your opponent on your way toward the ball and you may not touch your opponent's crosse in any way should she not be in possession of the ball. Both actions are infringements of the rules—not only on this occasion, of course, but at any time. Speed of 'get away' plus the ability to catch and twist quickly are of the utmost importance.

It is now necessary to deal more fully with the phrases, *"create a space"* and *"cut for a pass."* Remember if your team is in possession of the ball, you are being closely guarded by an opponent who is determined not to allow you a moment's freedom to receive a pass. First of all, you will have been instructed to head straight for goal when you have the ball, either to try to draw an opponent or as you look for someone in a better position than you to whom to pass. A ball can travel faster than a person can run, so *pass if you can.* But as a beginner there is also another problem created by several understandable factors.

In no other game can you enjoy the freedom of moving at top speed in possession of the ball. No matter how weary you might feel, suddenly the ball is yours and off you go. Perhaps your opponents are not yet skilled enough to body-check or crosse-check successfully, so you go on. Next you

37

are convinced that you need time to execute a pass, and so again you keep going. Third, the ability to find someone to pass to and to do so at the moment when she is free, only comes with practice. These three common problems, which result in holding on to the ball too long, are faced by all beginners and if you can recognize them early, it will help you to improve in *team play* that much sooner. Also, no player who constantly makes solo runs up and down the field can play her part as both an effective defense and attack player when needed.

Earlier you were reminded that in getting free for a pass there must be space into which you move. It is often necessary to *create this space!* This simply means that you attempt to draw your opponent away from the place where you wish to move to receive a pass. The player with the ball, though running toward goal, should have three choices of people she can pass to. You must be aware then where these other people are moving to, so that you and others will not all move into the same space. Constant alertness is a *must* in this game.

You must also remember that you may create a space, move into it, show yourself ready for a pass, and then not be used. Even though you think you should have been used, it is your teammate in possession of the ball who must make the decision regarding what to do with it.

By running as fast as you can to meet a ball coming toward you or to either side, you will also be creating a space. How? Picture your opponent also moving with you as you go to meet the ball. The distance that you move from the moment of receiving and controlling a pass will vary but as you move, tracked by an opponent, you will always leave a space. As you turn to head for goal, it is possible and indeed probable that a teammate may then move into this space to be ready for a pass should you wish to make it.

Having created the space, you should indicate with the crosse where you expect to receive the pass and then dart into the space. Cutting into the space is the logical follow-up of creating the space. Should you not be used, do not stand, but make another cut that might be useful to the pattern of play, or at least keep on the move so your opponent also will be kept occupied, never knowing your next plan, whether it be one of acting only as a decoy, or one with a definite purpose of further attack.

Often it is not possible for your first cut for a pass to be successful. Either your opponent is step-to-step with you, or perhaps you have moved too soon for the player with the ball to be able to use you. A final cut may well follow one or two feinting moves to throw your opponent off balance just long enough for you to get a head start into a space.

Remember that having created the space, having made the cut, you must also "ask" for the ball *away* from your opponent's crosse, otherwise she would be in an excellent position to intercept, or body check, or crosse-check. As you become more experienced you will find that all you need to be free is one stride and stretch ahead of your opponent. *If* the pass is *accurate,* you will be well away!

4

Positions

All players must have certain fundamental abilities and attributes upon which to build the specific requirements for each position. The abilities are those concerned with stickwork, footwork and speed. The attributes are concentration and understanding which combine to increase one's anticipation, and also the desire to learn about all positions, not only just one's own. To play both with and against the various positions with complete knowledge of the inherent problems and rewards of each requires the awareness of many factors.

GENERAL POINTS FOR ALL PLAYERS TO PRACTICE, REMEMBER AND PUT INTO PLAY

1. PASSING. Can you, while moving at top speed, pass the ball at the speed required to achieve the exact distance dictated by the situation? Sometimes the ball must travel in an arc-like path to arrive in a space at the same time as the player who is moving into the space. At other moments the ball must travel directly—short, quick and direct—from your crosse to your teammate's crosse at the moment she is free—devastating to an opponent! You must match the speed of the ball to the speed of the receiver. It is most important that you be able to pass to the left or to the right, as well as straight ahead.

2. CATCHING. Can you catch with equal ease on either side and at both high and low levels? Opponents will force you into situations which make it most necessary to acquire this ability.

3. PICKING UP A STATIONARY BALL. Can you, while running at top speed, get the ball on the first try? The most exhausting part of the game to any individual and the most frustrating to her teammates is a succession of unsuccessful attempts to get the ball off the ground. The game as well as the players bog down. It is vitally important to pick the ball up on the

first go. The great difficulty is of course that more often than not you will have an opponent equally intent upon getting the ball. Either beat her to it, or with your crosse, move it into a space away from her and get there before she does.

4. DEALING WITH A BALL COMING TOWARD YOU ON THE GROUND. Can you, as the ball comes either toward you or from either side, collect it into your crosse without breaking your speed of approach?

5. BODY CHECKING AND CROSSE CHECKING. As all players are defense at times, these skills are necessary to regain possession of the ball for your team. A combination of swiftness of foot and control of body and crosse are necessary if you are to play the game successfully and ensure the safety of all.

6. DODGING. Although a pass to a teammate is often the best dodge, there will be many times when either there is no one free to receive a pass, or a pass might be of little value. As a defense player, seeking to get the ball away, a dodge is often necessary before you can find a teammate to whom you could or should pass. As an attack player the above is also true but with it comes another situation. There may be only one opponent between you and the chance to shoot for goal. Wouldn't it be a pity if you lacked that necessary swiftness and deception of body and crosse and were therefore stymied in your efforts to achieve your purpose?—to score!

7. CROWDING. If the ball is on the ground, there should never be more than two people attempting to pick it up. To have more is both foolish and dangerous! Remember that these two players must have room in which to move themselves and the ball.

8. ANTICIPATION. This will be helped by watching the eyes of the player with the ball; they often give away, too soon, the intended direction of the pass.

9. SPEED. Always *move* to meet the ball coming toward you whether it is in the air or on the ground. Do not slow up as the ball enters your crosse—*accelerate instead.*

GENERAL POINTS FOR DEFENSE

1. YOUR DIRECT OPPONENT IS YOUR MAIN CONCERN. Determination plus concentration, added to the skill you are aiming to acquire, must combine to make you relentless in your efforts, never, if possible, to allow your opponent the freedom necessary to receive the ball.

2. INTERCEPTION IS THE KEY WORD IN ALL DEFENSE PLAY. However, to err is human and, also, your opponent will be equally determined. Practicing the timing for interception is necessary. One way to practice follows:

Get into a group of three, A, B and C. C's aim will be to cut between A and B. Have A pass the ball to B. You, as C, *move only* as the ball leaves A's crosse and see if you can intercept it on its flight to B. In the beginning have A and B stand still and place yourself a sensible distance from them, then gradually increase the distance that you must move in order to intercept. Next have them move toward you and, as they pass, nip in between them to try to gather in the pass. (Diagram F)

3. NEVER ALLOW YOUR OPPONENT TO GET GOAL SIDE OF YOU. Mark closely so that by acceleration or anticipation you can intercept or, should your opponent receive the ball, you are goalside of her ready to body check and crosse check.

4. TRY NEVER TO ALLOW YOUR OPPONENT TO BE FREE to receive the ball as she is heading toward goal. Mark so she must move away from the direct path to the goal to get free to receive a pass.

5. BE QUICK TO MOVE ONTO THE ATTACK when one of your defense gains possession of the ball. She may need *you* to help relay it to the attack.

6. YOU MUST BE ABLE TO THROW short passes and accurate long ones as well, in order for the ball to get to your attacking end of the field as quickly as possible.

7. ALWAYS BE AWARE of your other defense players and the possibility that one has been, or is about to be, passed by an opponent. Interchange will become necessary.

8. STICK TO-IT-IVENESS or glue-like tenacity in your body checking and crosse checking, though you may not actually retrieve the ball yourself, will worry and disconcert your opponent and may force her either to pass before she is ready or make her pass inaccurately. It will also slow her down in her run toward goal. The rest of your team, aware of these various outcomes, should be prepared to deal with the situation which you have forced.

9. SHOULD YOU BE THE PLAYER WHO MUST MOVE to take on a free player coming toward goal, do not run directly toward her or stand still. You will be easily dodged. Rather, approach her at an angle, ready to give back with her in the direction toward which she is moving as you body and crosse check.

10. GET ON TO ANY LOOSE BALL IMMEDIATELY.

11. KNOW THE RULES OF THE CREASE. Be quick to dart into the crease, particularly in that area behind the goal, to retrieve the ball. You can do it more easily than the goalkeeper; also it would be both quicker and safer for you to do it. As no attack player may enter the crease to get the ball, you have the advantage of at least momentary but secure possession.

The ability to think *and* act quickly is vitally necessary for a defense. Dithering is fatal, so is lack of stamina and absence of determination. Nimble, quick footwork allowing you to change direction rapidly or to accelerate, a body well-balanced over this darting quick-moving base, plus good stickwork, combined with initiative, spirit and enjoyment, will make the game intriguing, exciting and, at times exhausting.

DEFENSE WING. Your opponents are the two wing attacks, the very name conjuring in one's mind a picture of speed and action, and it is against these qualities that you must pit your energy. You are playing the most

By moving forward just as the ball leaves A's or B's crosse, can you intercept four, six, or eight passes out of ten? How many if A and B are moving toward you as they pass? Can you increase the distance you must run and still succeed?

Evaluation Questions

PRACTICING
PASS INTERCEPTION

active position on the field. Not only will you be well back on defense, wherever your opponent takes you, you may also have the opportunity to move well into the attacking half of the field. In fact you may even occasionally have a shot for a goal. Perhaps you have intercepted a pass midway up the field. As you move toward goal, looking for a teammate moving into a good position to pass to, you are for a moment a free player. The indecision of your opposing defense and the sudden spacing of your attack, as they realize the opportunity, may open the path toward goal for you.

The marking of your wing attack will not always be done with the same closeness as that of the other defense. Of course you mark closely on the center draw to prevent the ball from getting to your attack wing, or should she get it, you are "on her" immediately. Also, you mark closely if the play is on or coming down your side of the field. However, should the ball be coming down the center or on the opposite side of the field, you must move back on a level with second home. The reason for this is that should any member of the opposing team break free, cover point is the player most likely to come off her opponent. The defense wing then nearest to second home must take on this key member of the attack and stay with her. By moving back toward second home you will also be in a position to observe the pattern of play and be ready for it. You can see from this move that you are no longer marking your wing closely but you are still between her and your goal.

Never let your attack wing get goal side of you. It is a favorite trick that they like to try. If successful, the rest of your defense is momentarily in a very difficult position.

Try to intercept any pass from your opposing defense up to your attack wing. A wing, closely covered by her defense wing, is difficult to use in relaying the ball. Make sure that *your* opposing attack wing is difficult to

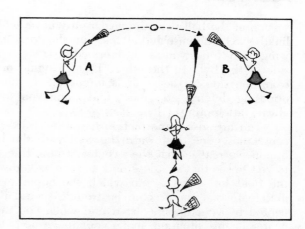

Diagram F:

**PRACTICING
PASS INTERCEPTION**

use. If, however, your attack wing has to move well into her defending half of the field to receive a pass from her defense, usually it is unwise for you to move up that far. Should you do so, the attack wing could turn and out-run you, either with the ball or as she turns to get free for a pass.

Be alert for any ball being passed from behind the goal toward your *own* opponent or even one of the other attacks. Be quick to pick up any loose ball near the goal and start it on its way toward your own attack. Should the goalkeeper or point or even cover point with the ball find it difficult to clear to your attack, make yourself available to help in its relay. Vary your passes. Though you would never pass directly across in front of the goal, further up the field look, not only for your own attack wing, but also for the center and your attack wing on the other side of the field and distribute passes in as varying a pattern as possible.

Yours is an exciting position for so much depends upon you and your constant movement. It is a position of great freedom in a way, but with this freedom comes the responsibility for not only your own opponent but the opponents of the other defense players, particularly second home. Your moves must be calculated and definite in their execution. The more you play the more you will become aware of the tremendous range of movement and initiative which is possible in this position.

THIRD MAN. Because of your position on the field in relation to both attack and defense you have the added attraction of occasionally being the initiator of the attack as well as being so vitally important to the defense. At the center draw you must be ready to intercept the ball coming toward third home. As play starts down the field either from the draw or from your opponents' end of the field, third home is most often the player to begin the pattern of play. She must not be left free, but marked closely, almost, crosse to crosse. When one of your own defense gains possession of the ball near the goal, you will be looked for as that connecting link between defense and attack. You should also be ready should a defense wing wish to use you as an intermediary receiver to send the ball from one side of the field to the other. This changing of the direction of the ball from one side to the other is important, if done quickly. Throwing your opposing defense off guard, and using you to help is often safer than always attempting a long pass.

You are also important in two very tricky situations: (1) Your own center has gone on toward the goal with the ball. She loses it and your opponents realize that their center is now free to receive a pass. It is up to you to see that she does not. As soon as your own center takes off down the field for a space into which she hopes to receive a pass, you must anticipate that there could be trouble should the ball be suddenly intercepted by your opponents. If and when you move to mark the opposing center in this situation, make your move definite so that cover point may move in time to mark your third home. (2) Should an opponent, free and with the ball, start down the middle of the field, if there is time and you have not been drawn too far afield by third home you must move to body and crosse check her. The move must not be too late, as the player with the ball will find your third home before cover point can mark her, nor must the move be too soon, before the defense wings can get back and cover point be ready.

After you have passed the ball, get back at top speed to mark your opponent. Like the defense wings, you have more room in which to move and to create an attack, but you also have the important responsibility of sometimes setting up the interchange of the defense. You have a vast area in which to be responsible for third home.

COVER POINT. This position demands excellent timing, fleetness of foot, acceleration and initiative as well as close, accurate stickwork. Your opponent, second home, is considered the pivot of the attack. To mark her out of the game is your main objective. But in addition, you are considered to be the pivot of the defense. You must be strong and decisive. Your anticipation and judgment are vitally necessary in achieving the cohesiveness of your entire defense. Strive for interception or quick checking before your opponent has control of the ball. The ability to make short, quick, accurate passes will pay dividends.

As well as being aware of the play as it moves toward your area, the pattern of the attack and the relative positioning of the defense, you must also know the positioning of your defense wings. Should you move too soon to take a free player before the defense wing is in position to cover for you, your second home is dangerously free in a vulnerable zone. Your battle will be a constant one: to mark second home adequately, and yet be wise in how far you must follow her, remembering that you are the one who must also be prepared to come off on a free player. All this takes practice, concentration and the ability to assess your opponents.

POINT. You are, except for the goalkeeper, the last of the defense. First home, your opponent, has been chosen for several reasons, one being that she can maneuver her body and her crosse quickly in a small space and needs little time between her catch and a shot for goal. Your abilities must match hers. You must mark her tenaciously and relentlessly and your concentration must be complete. If you try to intercept, you must be sure of success. Your body and crosse checking must be neat and accurate: there can be no retrieving of your mistake. How far do you follow your first home? Stay with her! A first home, free behind the goal or even fairly wide of it, can court disaster for your team because of her ability to set up plays. You must be able to intercept, to pick up rebounds from the goal-keeper's pads or crosse, to gather up any loose ball around the crease. You must have the ability to dodge successfully in a small and perhaps crowded area, and to pass accurately to one of your own team. It may sometimes be necessary for you to deputize for the goal keeper which means knowing her privileges. Never just place yourself in front of the goal. Not only will you unsight your goal keeper but should you get hit, you would have no one to blame but yourself.

It cannot be said that you never leave first home, but if ever you do, it is as a last resort. While marking first home, perhaps another player has broken free from the rest of your defense. Your decision must be quick as to whether to leave first home and attempt to body and crosse check the free player in an attempt to either to gain possession of the ball or to force a hurried shot or pass. Much will depend upon the distance you must travel to do so. Do you take the chance or not? If you can possibly prevent a player from having an absolutely free chance at shooting, your goal keeper would want you to try. It will be no good if you are caught part way between the two attacks. There can be little doubt about the outcome from this dilemma.

Your position demands sound technique and sound judgment. Both should and will come with practice.

GOALKEEPER. You truly are the last line of the defense but you can and should be also the starter of an attack. Your position is both one of giving confidence to your team and of the team giving confidence to you. At all times you must portray calmness despite what you may feel inside. Your defense, by their knowledge and performance in intercepting, body and crosse checking, and interchanging, should make your position easier and also more exciting. Rather than being left often at the mercy of the attack because of a poor defense, your position should be one of constant attack and not solely one of defense. This is only possible of course when you know that each member of the opposing attack is well and properly "taken care of."

Now what will make you a good goalkeeper? Courage, yes, but there is much more than that! All the techniques necessary to play on the field must also be yours, even the ability to accelerate, to dodge, and to body

*Figure 24—Goalkeeper
in ready Position*

and crosse check. These will be more difficult for you as you will be slightly hampered by your protective equipment. Well-fitting leg pads and a proper chest protector are absolutely essential. Unless you are playing against skilled attacks whose shooting is both controlled and accurate, it would be wise to wear a light-weight catcher's mask as well. If you wear glasses, the mask is a must. Since you are allowed to use your hands, a pair of gloves will give added protection. Both your body and your crosse will be used in the defense of your goal. Like any other player, you try to catch the ball no matter at what level or on which side it comes. Be sure to *watch the ball in the crosse of the shooter* and not her face. This takes absolute concentration. (Figure 24)

Every day do the stickwork practices done by the others. Sometimes play on the field instead of in the goal. This practice will help you perfect and speed up your stickwork and also will give you more understanding of the game, thus enabling you to better observe and react to the play as its patterns unfold.

To quicken your reactions and your footwork, you can give yourself valuable practice with a crosse, a ball and a wall. Vary the heights and the speed with which you shoot at the wall and move always behind the flight of the ball as it caroms back at you. After a shot has been made it is important to gather the ball into your crosse, rather than let it rebound. Don't bat at the ball or flick it. Avoid all of these mistakes, for in a game

46

an attack player will be ready to pounce on any such mistake and shoot again.

Your teammates *must* be willing to help you by giving you practice, such as:

1. *Long* bouncing shots aimed at just inside the crease from various angles in front of the goal, yet some distance from it. Move your body and your crosse behind the ball and bend slightly forward into it as it comes. Both of these actions are important. The body stops what the crosse might miss. Also if you get into the habit of retreating behind the ball, you may well make the error of stepping back over your goal line as you either gather in the ball or give with its impact, or, as you prepare to clear, you may take the ball in your crosse over the goal line. In both instances a goal would be scored.

2. Have your teammates cut back and forth across in front of the goal, popping the ball into its upper corners. In this case, some goalkeepers prefer to use their hands, particularly if the ball is high on your "non-stick" side. If you do catch it with your hand, you are allowed then to put it in your crosse. Try, however, to use your crosse to stop all shots, no matter at what height or on which side. The combination of a mobile body and crosse is safer than the palm of the hand, and a far better technique!

3. Your teammates should also place balls waist height to either side of you. This part of the goal is particularly difficult to defend. It may help to move your body to the opposite side of the goal from the flight of the ball. Here again a goalkeeper sometimes uses her hand to stop the ball on the "non-stick" side.

Your teammates must *never* shoot for goal with hard shots in practice, unless they are shooting with a defense against them. It is unfair and shattering to your confidence. With a defense against them you are more able to watch the movement of the crosse and the ball in the preparatory movement before the shot is taken. The practices suggested above are not only for the purpose of developing the accuracy of the players' attack but also to give you the opportunity to get your eye on the ball and to move your body in varying directions and the crosse at various levels as you defend your goal.

As well as catching or stopping the ball which is the defending function of your position, your "clear" to start an attack is equally important. A long and accurate pass is a most important part of your repertoire of skills. A pass to your wing attacks, who should not have to come back beyond the center of the field, is the length of throw you must aim to perfect. The throw must not be a loopy one as its flight takes longer and is therefore more easily intercepted. Having practiced the leverage and developed the strength necessary to propel the ball that distance, then practice with a defense against you. Rarely will you be able to clear the ball unhampered by an opponent. Though no player may enter the crease or have her crosse over the crease to check you, she can be most aggravating by moving all around the edge of the crease with her crosse moving to block the flight of your pass. If her movement is very effective and your own team closely marked up field, then you must look for assistance and 'clear' closer to goal. A sympathetic and understanding defense will recognize your plight and should move close enough so you can pass to one of them.

The crease is for your protection and it allows you to move in front, behind and beside your goal. Take advantage of it. On your long 'clears,' for instance, a faked movement indicating a long pass up one side of the field can be followed by a second move which takes you to the other side where you can release the ball in that direction. Don't always use the same side, or the same player to receive your clear. In addition to using your attack wings, notice if your center or even third man is free, and make use of them.

As play goes on behind your goal, be sure you can see what is happening. An opponent may be coming around with the ball to try for a shot, quite free. Should you move out to crosse check or not? This decision will have to be made quickly and will depend upon how close to the crease she is and whether or not one of your teammates is ready to cope with her. In another case your opponent is about to pass to a teammate moving into shooting position. Is the pass close enough for you to intercept? Perhaps one of your own defense has the ball and is being so well body checked that she cannot get free to get rid of the ball up the field. By being to the side of or behind your goal, you may be the one person who can receive the ball and you, in turn, can then start it on its way.

Should you gain possession of the ball after going out of your crease to crosse check or to intercept, you may not return to its protection until you have gotten rid of the ball. It is here that your ability to dodge and swerve is of the greatest importance. Encumbered by leg pads and body protector, you must have even more agility than your teammates. (Figure 25)

Figure 25—An Agile goalkeeper preparing to clear

You have now tried some simple practices to get your eye on the ball. You have learned the importance of both your body and your crosse in defending the goal and also of your movement around the goal, within the crease and out of it. Now about the goal you are actually defending. It is six feet square and every bit of it is used by the attack—they will always aim for the space you have left unguarded, probably one of the four corners or either side of you at waist height.

As the attack moves forward to shoot, your movement from side to side must not be in a direct line just in front of the goal line. Rather you move in a semi-circular or arc-like path, thereby decreasing the available angles. Watch someone move both straight across and then in an arc-like path and observe for yourself how space is decreased. With your foot or your hand or your crosse, constantly check your distance from either goal post. Should you anticipate that the ball will be shot from the left, then close against the left post you must be, the angle of your body slightly turned to face the direction of the ball. (Figure 24)

Any ball that is aimed at the ground to bounce or slither past you will react according to the ground conditions. These conditions you must assess if possible before the game begins. If the ground is dry or frozen, the bounce will be hard, fast and not true; if soggy or wet, it will slow down or stick in the ground or possibly slide on the wet grass at an incredible pace. Move quickly but do *not* jump to get behind the flight of the ball.

Yours is an exacting position, one of great responsibility, yet full of excitement, for no patterns of play are ever the same. A calm, apparently unruffled goalkeeper with courage, anticipation and concentration, with the ability to catch or stop any reasonable shot for goal and clear it accurately, will be greatly admired and respected by her teammates; such a goalkeeper often makes the difference between success and failure. With practice and determination your contribution will be immeasurable. Be sure you know the rules of the crease and your privileges. Remember that you even start with the respect of your team for being willing to accept the role of goalkeeper.

GENERAL POINTS FOR ATTACK

Using the space available to its fullest advantage without sending ball and player too far afield is both your challenge and your problem. All attack positions must be aware of this as they cut and re-cut, creating spaces in which to move to receive the ball. Using space wisely will create problems for your opponents. If attacks are closely marked, as they should be, and in your moves you tend to converge on one another, you make it far easier for your opponents to interchange to the player who might break free. Your spacing must make this distance and interchange a worry for the defense aginst you. All too often in the beginning stages it is easy for the defense "to step" quickly from one to the other of the attacks, which

49

makes intercepting simpler. Remember that what might appear to be a large space may be quickly reduced between the time a player cuts at full speed for the ball and receives and controls it. With lots of practice this catch and control will be accomplished in one or two movements, but with this skill there must also be the ability to combine space and speed.

1. Once in possession of the ball, head straight for goal, ready to go on or pass according to the situation.

2. Should one of your teammates get free and have a clear path toward goal, do not cross her path or move in any direction that will allow your opponent to get close to her.

3. If one of your attacks is closely body and crosse checked, it will be difficult for her to make a pass straight ahead, so do not think that you will help her to get rid of the ball if you run away from her to ask for a pass, particularly if you too are closely marked. Any pass to you in this situation will be intercepted easily. Use another direction instead which will provide an easy path for a pass from your teammate, and cut in such a way that you make a pass from your teammate possible.

4. Running directly toward a player with a ball or diagonally toward her is often wise if she will let you have the ball in time. By moving in either of these directions you have the advantage of having momentarily outwitted your opponent. She will, of course, be in hot pursuit, but you will have then made a space for another teammate to move into, or for the player who has passed you the ball to move into, ready to receive a return pass. (Figure 26)

5. As you often will have to receive the ball with your back or your side to the goal you are attacking, *the ability to turn or pivot quickly, to be followed either by a pass or a sprint toward goal,* is most important.

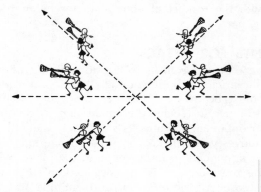

Figure 26—Possible Angles to move when cutting for a pass.

6. Too often, players tend to look only straight ahead for a team-mate moving to receive a ball. A *good player* will look toward the center of the field as well. The ability to look left and right for a free player will make for a variety of passing and therefore make the defense's work more difficult.

7. It is absolutely vital, should you be the attack nearest the goal at the time the goalkeeper has the ball in her crosse ready to make a clear, that you make yourself a nuisance by moving around the crease following her moves and trying to intercept the pass with your crosse.

8. Be ready to pounce on any ball rebounding from the goalkeeper's stick or pads, and shoot.

9. Should you be on your way to goal, be aware of where your other attacks are. You undoubtedly will not be allowed to be free for long. Some defense player must move to "take you on." The timing of your pass then becomes most important. One of your objectives for running on is to try to draw a defense. One of the important reasons for the spacing of the attacks is to make the distance that the defense must move away from her own opponent to the free player as great as possible. The pass, then, must be made at the time when this next attack player is left free and before another defense moves in to take her, as this attack will be the next source of danger to the defending team. Do not wait until you are close enough to your opponent to be body and crosse checked.

10. Shooting is the culmination of the attack. Accuracy plus variety must be acquired. Draw a goal on a wall, or better still, place pieces of paper in the four corners of a goal to use as targets. Vary the intensity of your shots and also vary your approaches, moving toward the goal, across it or coming around the crease from behind the goal. Always be concerned with the position of your body and your crosse in relation to the crease, particularly on the follow through of your shot. Remember that even though your ball may go into the net the goal will be disallowed if any part of your body or crosse goes over the crease following your shot. Have a part-ner pass a ball to you as you run at top speed and work for the perfection of catching and shooting in one action.

The four corners of the goal and the area at waist height are the most difficult for the goalkeeper, so practice with this in mind. "Willy-nilly" shooting is of no use to you or your team.

Be the type of goal shooter who is respected because of her considera-tion, and feared for her accuracy. Never shoot hard high shots at the goal-keeper nor through any defense who may be between you and the goal. Never be the kind of attack who, either lacking ability or concern for others, can score goals by thoroughly intimidating a goalkeeper. Scoring goals in this fashion should never give one a feeling of a job well done or any sense of satisfaction. Of course, you will shoot hard at times, many times, but these shots should be either the long hard bouncing shots with a definite downward action, or the underarm shots which start low and end low.

Shots into the upper corners are accomplished with but a *flick of the wrists*, the direction of the shot being governed by the amount of twist through the shoulders and by the path of the crosse during the execution. In making these high shots, your actions might portray speed, your facial expression might be intense, but the flight of the ball must be "*soft.*" The very change of pace is difficult for a goalkeeper to react to.

In England there is now a rule which gives the umpire the right to disallow any shot which she considers dangerous to the goalkeeper. Although this places the umpire in a difficult position, the rule is an excellent one.

There is no use practicing shooting with no opponent against you. To be accurate while moving quickly and at the same time to be almost engulfed by an opponent is far more difficult. Frustration from the latter in a game leads to bad and uncontrolled shooting.

Practice a high catch followed by a high easy shot, a high catch followed by a hard low shot, a lower catch or pickup followed by either a high or a low shot. The ability to do all these well will prove invaluable.

CENTER. You are the link between the defense and the beginning of the attack. You never stop running. Not at top speed at all times, but the nature of the game, and the speed with which the ball may go from one end of the field to the other, as well as "change hands," so to speak, means that your position of "up and back," as well as from attack to defense, is an ever changing one. Your role must be, above all, never to let your opposing center be free when her team has the ball. A free center on the attack can be wearying, frustrating and dangerous to the defense. Now knowing this, *you* will try to break free from your opposing center when your team has the ball. Should the ball be coming from your defense you must make yourself available for a clear. It is sometimes impossible for members of your defense to find an attack wing free, also it is unwise for a defense always to use the same pattern of play in clearing the ball up the field. Both of these situations make it imperative for you to time your move for the pass at the moment the player with the ball is ready to pass. You know also of the importance of changing the pattern of play from one side of the field to the other—here too you are a link.

On the attack you may either have gained possession of the ball and be running through toward goal or you may see a space right into which to move to receive a pass. Should the fortunes of play suddenly change, you must streak back to mark your opposing center, or to try to intercept any long pass that might be attempted by your opposing defense up to their wing attacks or their center. Intercepting these long passes, and never allowing your opposing center to be free enough to receive the ball from her defense, should keep you very busy on the defense, and connecting the field from defense to attack as well as from side to side should challenge your attacking instincts. Your part in the game is continuous and undoubtedly exhausting. Your contribution to the two sides of any game

—defense and attack—can be exciting, sparkling and rewarding. It is necessary for you to perfect your draw, trying always to get the ball to your wing attack, or if the wing defense is being much too successful in intercepting, then you should try to get the draw to third home.

WING ATTACKS. Yours is a terrific position, one that adds to the speed and to the spread of the game, as well as to the scoring of goals. In the beginning you might well choose it because of the comparative freedom of movement it offers in relation to the other attacks—you are not always as closely marked as they and you love to run. But you must also be ready and eager to score goals. Because you have more freedom of movement and at times are more loosely marked is no excuse for sloppy stickwork. Your ability to catch, pivot, pass, or to catch and shoot, will determine your success as an attack wing.

To begin with, your part in the game commences immediately with the word "draw." Your center attempts to direct the ball to you, particularly if you are the left attack. Good anticipation and a successful catch will start your team on its way. Even as you are about to catch the ball, your center, your three homes and your other attack wing will be on the move to make themselves available for a pass. All too often a wing attack *tends to look only straight ahead* for a receiver. A quick glance might well find your other wing attack, having seen you gather in the ball, outrunning her wing defense and ready to receive a well placed pass ahead of her and into the space. This pass must be done quickly before the wing defense adjusts to the situation. You may also see your center, who has suddenly moved into the space left by the homes, spacing for the attack. Though the above refers to the draw, the reminders are meant for any occasion in which you have the ball, or when you are the wing attack on the opposite side of the field. Beware of always looking for second home as the person to receive your pass for the defense soon "cotton on" to favorite passes and "passing patterns."

Should the ball go to any other member of your team on the draw, immediately pull away from the center of the field, and try to get ahead of your defense wing. You might well have a difficult time achieving this but that doesn't mean that you give up trying.

If the ball is moving down the center of the field, stay out and on a level with the play. Your two defense wings, as you know, have now dropped away from you and are on a level with second home. By staying well out, you will avoid crowding your homes and also it may be easier to drop behind your wing defense who is having to observe your movements as well as those of cover point. A moment of indecision on her part can be turned into an advantage for your team. Also if well out, you are available to receive a pass which may well be used by you as the set up for a further pass down the field. If you "keep your distance," not only making yourself free for use but also giving your homes more space in which to move, you will many times observe that opportunity when you

53

should ask for the ball as you head for the space from where you can shoot. Sometimes this chance will come some distance from goal and in this case you must use your long hard bouncing shot. At other times you will see a space into which you may move which will take you across in front of the goal, where an accurate pass *to* you and a quick shot *by* you might well result in a score. You must be cautioned from the beginning to avoid crowding in toward the goal for you will ruin the movements of your homes. Also you will bring your defense wings in on top of your homes as well. Better stay out, observe the pattern of the play and pounce on your chance when it comes.

On the attack, always be ready to retrieve balls from behind the goal or help in relaying the ball back into a possible shooting angle. Also, once the ball has been intercepted by your opponents, move back quickly to see if you can intercept any passes to your opposing wing defense or wing attack.

Your part in the attack can also begin when a member of your defense has the ball. You must have already made your way back quickly as far up the field as the center circle. Your defense will expect to find you moving to receive a clear from them in this area at least. A defense will also try not to make you come much farther than the halfway mark by getting a quick long pass off to you, if you cut at the right moment for a pass. However, if the defense is very hard pressed by their opponents, their ability might be somewhat limited. This may mean that you have to retreat farther into your defending area to help. Should this be necessary, upon catching the ball, you must turn quickly and make an immediate pass if possible, and it should be possible, as the other attacks should be ready to cut immediately upon your turn.

It can be said that generally you should ask for the ball going away from the center of the field either straight to the side, diagonally forward or diagonally away. This leaves your wing defense a little closer to the center of the field. If you are the right attack, and you play right hand up, you will be asking for the ball on the side of your bottom hand. As you receive the pass, you will then be bringing your crosse over to your right as you make half a turn to head for goal. Also your crosse is in position to execute an immediate shoulder pass to a cutting teammate. If you are the left attack, as you gather in the ball, your immediate quick pass could be an underarm pass should your wing defense be on you. In both cases you will have received the ball with your shoulder between your opponent and your crosse.

It was mentioned earlier that perhaps one of the reasons for your choosing to be a wing attack might be your love of running. However, you must always remember that your ability to find an attack to whom to pass will make the passage of the ball toward the goal not only more rapid but also more effective, particularly when in possession of the ball in the defending half of your field or even halfway up the field. Farther down the field if free, by all means streak toward goal until you draw an opponent.

If you continually insist upon carrying the ball as long as you can, your ability to get down the field on attack as far as is necessary for you to go and then be back on defense will be lessened, thus diminishing your contribution to the team—fifty minutes of fast running covering an area more than fifty yards in each direction will be impossible. Remember you are not just a *fetcher* of the ball from the defense and a *carrier* of the ball to the attack.

Your position, combining the use of good stickwork with the ability to assess the movements of the center and the homes in relation to you and the goal, can be tremendously satisfying.

THIRD HOME. You are the initiator of the movement of the other homes both at the center draw and as the play comes down the field from the defense. In both of these situations your other two homes watch for the move you make. It may be toward the player with the ball, to the side the player with the ball is approaching, or to the opposite side. Their beginning spacing will in a way depend upon your moves. Once the ball has passed beyond your area and moved down toward the goal, your moves will depend upon the other homes and the attack wings. Your place is similar to that of center. You must be constantly aware of center. Should she be down near the goal when fortune has suddenly given the ball to your opponents, you must immediately make the opposing center your responsibility so that she is not free to receive a clearing pass. Should the gap between your defense and your attack become too great, then you must help relay the ball through this gap. Perhaps center has been drawn well to the side, in which case you must be ready to assist by showing yourself as willing and able to help in moving the ball from one side of the field to the other, by taking on this central area of the field. If your opponents have gained possession of the ball, you must get back quickly and try to intercept any clearing pass.

"Give and go" or triangular passes between you and your attack wings will often help the attack wing to get by her defense wing. For example, your wing attack has the ball and is about to be body checked. If you move in time, a quick pass should come to you and then the attack wing should flash by her defense wing and be ready to receive the ball back again. "Give and go" can be also very effective between you and the second home, or you and the first home. (Diagram G)

Having read about third man, your opponent, you realize how important her decision is as to whether or not to come off on a free player coming down the center of the field. Part of your job then, if you see this situation developing, is to move so the distance your opponent must travel makes her job more difficult. Should she leave you, you are free for a pass. If she stays with you, then you have created a lovely space for the free player to move into.

Despite your seemingly central position on the field and its link between attack and defense, the ability to move in a small space and to shoot are as important for you as for the other homes.

SECOND HOME. You are the pivot of the attack matching wits against your opponent, cover point, who is the pivot of the defense. And what a battle of wits, speed, anticipation and reaction it should be! Why called the pivot of the attack? Regardless of where the ball is, your position should allow you to take in at a glance the movements of the other five attacks and fit yourself into the pattern of play. As you become better and better in your position you will be able to visualize the pattern perhaps two passes ahead. Ability to cover a large area with speed and to move quickly and safely with sudden changes of direction within a small space, plus competence in dodging and shooting while closely marked are the qualities that you must strive to attain. With quick accurate passes you will often be the "play maker." By receiving and giving the ball back you will have the chance to set up those moves which will lead to the opportunity to shoot.

You may well set up plays in quite another context. Since your oponent is the pivot of the defense then it must also be your task to make her position more difficult. Being the pivot of the defense means that she, more often than not, must make the initial move to take on one of your attack players who has escaped her defense. Your effectiveness in this situation will depend upon the speed of your reaction with reference to what is about to happen or is happening. As you size up the possible breakthrough, you must move with the intent of making her change more difficult, both from the distance and the direction point of view. The timing of your move must be carefully done to increase the uncertainty of cover point as to whether your move means you intend to ask for the ball or you are putting on a ruse to distract her attention and change her intention. Remember also that wing defense nearest you will take you on as her opponent should cover point leave. Your awareness then of the wing defenses is also important, whether you are setting up the play by passing, or setting it up by momentarily becoming an unpredictable decoy.

Your position requires excellent stickwork and footwork combined with a keen and imaginative mind.

FIRST HOME. Primarily a shooter of goals, and the ever moving, unpredictable worrier of point and the goalkeeper. A fairly wide area all around the goal is yours, but of course it is shared with other attacks as you "give way" should the pattern of play or the position of your opponents make you expendable for the moment.

First home must have, in addition to all the stickwork expected of others, the ability to perform in a small space. Your movements must be *neat and quick*. You must be able to pick up in a flash any rebounds from the goalkeeper's pads or crosse. You must learn to shoot as you approach from any angle or direction. Your shots must be varied and disguised. It is

56

your job also, because you are the one most likely to be near the crease, to try to prevent the goalkeeper from clearing accurately or, should she come out of her crease with the ball, you must take her on as your opponent.

Remember that the area in front of the goal, approximately ten yards in radius, should be kept free for you or any attack to move into to receive a pass and shoot. You and second home are the most freqeunt users of this space and neither should linger there. Your cuts into it must be quick and well timed to receive the pass you expect. If not seen or used, you must continue your cutting, darting movements. You must practice catching and shooting in one motion, particularly high catches and shots near goal.

Of all the attacks, you are most closely marked. Point will try never to lose you, and your opposing defense will try their utmost never to have a situation in which point must decide to leave you to take on a free player about to shoot. However, no defense is infallible! This situation will arise and your immediate recognition of it is fundamental. Move so that point is taken as far as possible from the oncoming player, yet move yourself to a position in relation to the goal, where, during the moment of point's change over to take on the free player, you can receive the pass and shoot. All of this must be done with perfect timing and speed.

Your moves and cuts must always be aimed to allow you to receive the ball as you head toward goal if possible. Making your cuts too wide will of course limit the objective of your playing first home—that of scoring goals.

5

Attack
and Defense Play

You have studied the various positions and their special qualifications, each having the basic demands of quick, neat footwork, the ability to throw and catch accurately while moving at top speed, and the knack of combining with your teammates in both *thought and action.* The keen player will not only understand her own position but also the demands and the responsibilities of the others as well. In so doing she will become a more sympathetic team member, anticipating the play. Combining with others in planning and outwitting one's opponents results in a pleasure that is quite indescribable and is only realized by those who have succeeded. The playing of any game should not end with merely sheer physical weariness; there should be a mental weariness as well. This is the proof of complete concentration, of maximum effort, of having used all your powers of anticipation, quick decision and action.

You have both read and experienced the delight and freedom of this game. Marvellous, yes! but how does one use this freedom wisely? How can one use the space to its fullest advantage and have the ball travel in as direct a path as possible from one goal to the other?

ATTACK PLAY. The object in any game is to score goals. There will be moments when you will have the opportunity to be an individual and you must not then be afraid to be one. However, these moments are few. It is the *welding together* of six attack players that makes a team. Each attack player is a goal shooter and each of you will want to be one, a most natural ambition! However, it takes little imagination to picture the crowding and chaos, if each attack player is determined to shoot: there must be a constant awareness of five others. There are three basic points to remember if you are to avoid crowding: (1) Always be on the move when you receive a pass or when you are shooting; (2) If you have made a cut to receive a pass and you are not used, keep moving both to clear a space

58

and to take your opponent with you; (3) Always leave about a ten yard radius free in front of the goal into which you or a teammate may move to receive a pass and shoot.

One of the most basic and devastating ways to get by or through a defense is a pass, called by some a triangular pass, by others a "give and take" pass, or a "give and go" pass. You have learned about dodging an opponent as you carried the ball. You know it is wise to pass if possible, and if opportune. This new maneuver combines the pass and the getting by. Imagine yourself with the ball about to be body checked and crosse checked. A teammate seeing this moves quickly either left or right asking for the ball. An immediate pass to her, followed by a burst of speed from you around your opponent and into the space left by your teammate, will make you free to receive the ball back again as you head for goal. This simple pass should be practiced over and over with a partner. Place the ball on the ground. Run, pick it up, and immediately when you have the ball in control look for your partner who should be ahead of you, waiting to move at top speed. When she sees you have control, she should move either left or right. Pass the ball immediately and run behind her (or into the space she has left) and expect the ball to be passed back instantly. Should your partner move from left to right she will receive the ball and return it with a shoulder pass even as her feet continue in the direction she is going. If she moves from right to left, her return pass to you will be an underarm pass. It should be as close as possible to the phrase "catch, pass." (Diagram G)

This particular basic pass may illustrate more clearly one of the reasons for creating a space. You have read about and practiced cutting and creating spaces; now is the time to combine these ideas and practices with four or possibly five other attack players. The reasons for creating spaces are: (1) To make a space to move into yourself to receive a pass; (2) To make a space for a teammate to move into to receive a pass; (3) To make a space for the player with the ball to move into. In the triangular pass described above, two different plans were carried out: (1) The player with the ball, by passing to her teammate, made a space for herself to move into to receive the return pass; (2) The player who cut and "asked" for the ball, made a space for her teammate to move into.

Consider also the path of the ball in this particular case. Though the player moved in a straight line, the ball moved in a zigzag pattern. Can you now picture the moves of players and the passing which would make the ball travel in a straight line while the players moved in zigzag paths? Take the three homes as an example. Imagine third man or center about to receive the ball, third and first homes have moved to one side and second home to the other side, all homes thereby leaving the center space of the field toward goal quite open. As the center or third man receives and controls the ball, third home darts back into the space she has left and receives the ball; as she catches it, second home moves back into the space

Do you know three names for this maneuver? Which pass should your partner use to return the ball to you if she moves from right to left?

Evaluation Questions

COMBINING A PASS AND DODGE

she has left for herself and receives the next pass, then first home cuts back into the space she has left, receives the next pass and shoots. Can you picture the darting, cutting moves of the homes and the ball being passed in its *straight path from one to the other* in its flight toward goal? Of course to have the ball move as directly as possible toward goal is ideal, but opponents and circumstances dictate the pattern of play. As no situation is ever completely repeated, the ability to capitalize on opportunities as they arise makes or breaks the purpose of any game—to score goals. Often the ball must travel in a most indirect path as spaces must be created for players to cut into in order eventually to move the ball to within shooting distance of the goal.

An attack player may require but one move to get free to receive a pass but usually she may have to make several initiating movements before she can lose her opponent long enough to receive the ball. Considering this fact and, using only the two attack wings and the three homes, the number of moves and counter moves that could be planned in an attack would be infinite in number and kaleidoscopic in changing patterns. Set plays have no place in this game. Ingenuity, imagination, sympathy and awareness must work at all times to create problems for the defense.

When and how to move of course comes with experience. The right moment to make a move to receive a pass is so dependent upon the ability of the player with the ball. The ability to catch a ball, control and pass it, in almost one movement comes with time and practice. Your assessment of the player who has just received the ball is important. Is she enough "in possession of the ball" to pass? Should you make your final move too soon your efforts will be wasted. Your opponent, though perhaps momentarily left, will have now caught up. The word "empathy" is important in this matter of timing.

Diagram G:

COMBINING
A PASS AND DODGE

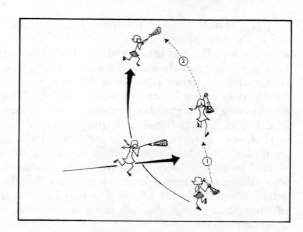

HOMES.   There are no hard and fast rules regarding your moves. The more you play, and play with the same people, the more you will become aware of their movements and their capabilities. However, if you can remember at least in the beginning stages some basic thoughts and understand the reasons for them, the foundation for later play will be laid. First of all, try to think of yourself as one of the three points of a triangle and whatever your moves are, always be aware of the other two. As soon as the ball is on its way to one, the other two must be adjusting their positions for the next move. Now the size of the triangle is important. As Margaret Boyd stated it, "Imagine yourselves attached by an elastic band. The band can stretch and stretch but must never be allowed to slacken." Remember also that there are not just three of you really but six (your three opponents). The space needed to move at top speed, then to receive the ball, control it and pass, or perhaps pivot and pass, still at top speed, is considerable.

Though there are not any set plays, it will be time well spent practicing in threes, moving, catching, passing and moving again. Passes must be quick and direct in their flight.

Starting with the center draw, or as the ball progresses from your defense towards the attack, the homes begin their moves to create spaces. It would be impossible for all attack players to go at top speed at all times when the ball is at their end. The initiating and perhaps even the second move are calculated to throw your opponent off balance but your final cut to receive a pass must be done at top speed. Where this final cut is made depends upon the other attack players too. It is not to be ssumed that first home never moves away from that area near the goal. On the contrary, when the ball is midfield, it is first home who can most easily watch the moves of her attack wings and the other two homes. There is no reason why she should not cut up toward a wing attack who has the ball. In so doing she has created a space for one of the other homes or even the other attack wing. On the other hand as the play moves nearer the goal it may be center or third home who more clearly sees the moves of the attack wings and the other two homes. The opportunity may well present itself for third home or center to cut toward goal for a pass. Perhaps it would be easier in the beginning to think of the homes as A, B and C rather than first home, second home and third home. What is important to remember is that *not* all three homes move toward the goal simultaneously. Simple examples: (1) Should third home move toward goal and be used, her place should be immediately taken by another home, thus avoiding crowding and also taking a defense player away from the shooting area. (2) Should an attack wing cut in for a pass it would be wise for a home to move out. By moving back *or* out she will once again be creating a space for herself or a teammate.

ATTACK WING.   Once the ball has passed midfield, stay on line with the play, though well to the side. It is vitally necessary that you should always be ready and free for a pass. You might be needed to draw the defense and thereby open a space for one of your homes, or else if all the homes have moved to one side, there may be that wonderful opportunity for you to cut into the space left by them, to receive a pass and shoot. But you must also be aware of the possible move of the *center* who, seeing the area suddenly free down the center of the field, may make her bid for a pass.

In attack play, the player with the ball should have *three* or at least *two* choices of receivers. She decides which to use or whether to go on herself. Should she choose to pass, you will *know immediately* whether the ball is meant for you or a teammate. If not for you, you must change your mind, which might involve a change of direction or speed; alter your plan so you are ready for the next cut. This is very important not only so that you are prepared to continue to take part in the attack but also so that you occupy the complete attention of your opponent whose aim is to try to stay with you. Sometimes your initial moves will have as their only intent to keep your opponent unsure.

It would be impossible to describe all the moves for five or six attack players. Only by playing will you discover the many patterns that can and will evolve. This fact makes each game exciting and stimulating.

It must be remembered that when five or six attack players are mentioned here the actual play involves ten or twelve players—each of your opponents who are shadowing you. Because you, the attack player, hold the "upper hand" initiating the moves, the defense must thwart your attack. This may require a system of interchange. Should one of your teammates get free, the moves you make must draw your own opponent away in order to make such interchanging more difficult. This requires a constant awareness of spacing. It is important to create a problem for the defense, not

62

Which players normally take part
in the basic defense interchange?

Evaluation Questions

alleviate it—by always threatening your opponents when your team is *on the attack*. To maintain an attack encompasses more than merely having possession of the ball. It means also that *should* your opponents intercept the ball, you must immediately become defense minded, mark closely, body check and crosse check, and regain the ball if possible while it is still in your attacking end.

To play well as an attack you must also have the ability to defend.

DEFENSE PLAY. Now having some basic ideas for the attack, you should be aware of the problems which face you, the defense. Be determined to accept the challenges with which you will be constantly dealing. Determination and anticipation, relentless marking and body checking, will help create a formidable defense. The attack has the upper hand. Should they use space wisely and to its fullest advantage, your task of marking, intercepting, etc., will not be an easy one. You must stay with your opponent but not be drawn so far afield that you can be left behind. Even though the attack in a way can think ahead of you, you must be fast enough not only to shadow your opponent but also to seize the opportunity to break up the move. Also realize that you too have an advantage. Your position, always slightly goal side of your opponent, means that you can observe her, the player the ball, the position and perhaps the predicament of your fellow defense players. This observational advantage will help you to anticipate the moves of your oppoents and to be more successful in intercepting or interchanging. No defense player can be completely infallible, but neither can a single person be a whole defense—an attack player will "break through" with the ball. Here is when timing of your interchange is so important—yours and your fellow defense players. When a member of the defense has been passed, the next move involves more than just the one who moves in to take the free player. The minds and reactions of all the

63

defense are put to the test. A good defense player doesn't see her teammate in trouble after or even as she is outwitted or out-run—she sees it *when it is about to happen*. At this moment the defense must begin. Sympathy and empathy moulds a defense into being impregnable or as close to it as is possible. You will remember that a free player with the ball should go on until she draws another opponent. Her moment to pass the ball to the next free player is of vital importance to her team *as well as to yours*. If you take on the free player (interchange) you must be confident that your own opponent will not become the next source of danger. Your decision must be absolute and quick so your teammate may also move at the proper moment. Indecision leads to chaos!

So far we have dealt only with circumstances in which you are on the defense. Now let us be more positive. You have the ball. A good attack is the best defense, of course. Once in possession of the ball each of you becomes a member of the attack. Should *you* have the ball, increase your speed and be alert for your opponents who will be determined to get it back. Your task is to get the ball to one of your attack wings or to your center with a quick and accurate pass so that the ball will reach your attacking half of the field. All the defense must be prepared, by making sensible moves, to help you if necessary to relay the ball up the field. By sensible is meant moving in such a way that you must not have to pass the ball across the goal where it may be intercepted, but moving quickly instead into spaces before your opponents have readjusted from attack to defense. Each defense player must realize that her task is not over *until* the ball has reached the attack. Too often when one member of the defense gains possession of the ball, the others give a sigh of relief that the panic is over and pause in their efforts. They appear not to realize the difficulty the player with the ball might be having as she tries to execute a pass. It is almost impossible to make a long accurate pass when hampered by an opponent, and a poorly executed long pass will undoubtdely be intercepted. Back comes the ball!

This game, like any other team game, is built on the simple principle of attack versus defense. The techniques are the tools of the individuals participating and the team work is the sharing of responsibility—the give and take of opportunities gained and lost and gained again, the complete understanding of the role each is playing, and the ability to capitalize at once upon a mistake made by an opponent. In lacrosse, almost more than any other game, spacing is the main problem for both attack and defense, because of the lack of restrictions encountered in every other game, namely boundary lines and an offside rule. Only by perfecting your "tools" and by playing with a keen awareness of the game as a whole will you begin to enjoy this game to its fullest. It is not the player or the team that can run the fastest that will be the superior one. It is the team that combines its speed with good technique and, above all, the ability to think.

6

Rules of the Game

Various rules have repeatedly been mentioned because of their importance in relation to the skill or the action being described. Rules cannot be separated from techniques and certain aspects of play. This chapter is not a substitute for the *Official Hockey and Lacrosse Guide.* Here we will nearly gather together the main points. The Official Guide should always be consulted to find possible rule changes, the interpretation of rules, and also for the helpful articles and hints it always contains.

The rules of lacrosse are few and simple and easily understood. In a game where every player plays in a sensitive and controlled fashion, and this should be in every game, whistle blowing is conspicuous by its absence, the continuity and flow of the game being a delight to player and spectator alike.

The game is, contrary to other games, started by the words either "draw" or "play" and the whistle is used only to stop the play. Unless a goal has been scored, at the sound of the whistle all players must stand and may not move again unless directed by the umpire, until play is restarted. The words "play" or "draw" are usually prefaced by "ready," a preparatory guide to all players.

Should the ball become lodged in your crosse immediately stop and bang your crosse on the ground to try to dislodged it. If you are successful you carry on.

The fouls on the field outside the crease relate to body contact, rough or uncontrolled checking, playing a person's crosse when she is not in possession of, or handling the ball, this privilege being reserved to [only that of] the goalkeeper. No player may push or charge a player whether she is in possession of the ball or not. Such contact might occur when (1) A player either makes an unsuccessful dodge or is unskilled in dodging and so charges or pushes against her opponent in her effort to move forward; (2) A player, slow on her feet, uses her body to push against her opponent who has the ball; (3) A player *holds* her crosse *against* an opponent who is trying to dodge past; (4) In attempting to pick up a ball, a player trips or pushes her opponent off the ball or places her legs in such a way that her opponent is prevented from trying to get the ball; (5) During a throw-on, one player pushes or leans into her opponent as both move toward the oncoming ball.

Illegal checking means swinging or striking one's crosse roughly or recklessly up or down on an opponent's crosse. Instances could be: (1) A crosse which comes down on a hand or head; (2) A check with one hand only; (3) A hard uncontrolled check up or down. It is also illegal for a player to reach over the shoulder of her opponent when tackling from behind.

A player may not guard her crosse with a raised elbow or with one hand off the crease; nor may she dangerously flip the ball off the ground in any way to endanger her opponent; she may not throw her crosse under any circumstance.

No player may hold the ball on the ground with her crosse; she must continue to play it. Nor may she hold her opponent's crosse down.

Interference with a player's crosse when she is about to catch a ball whether on the ground or in the air, is not allowed.

Only the goalkeeper is allowed to handle the ball and no player is allowed to propel the ball with her foot intentionally.

For any infringement of the above rules, a free position is awarded to the opposing team on or near the spot of the infringement. No free position may be taken within ten yards of the goal and no player may be within five yards of the player taking the free position. If a foul is so severe that in the umpire's mind a goal most likely would have otherwise been scored, all opponents except the goalkeeper are moved out of the path of the player having the free position.

Should two opponents foul each other (a double foul), a draw is taken on the spot or near it. No draw maybe taken closer than ten yards to the goal and no player may be within five yards. A draw is also taken: (1) When an accident occurs though no foul has been committed; (2) When a ball becomes so stuck in a crosse that tapping on the ground does not dislodge it; (3) When the ball becomes stuck in a player's clothing; (4) When the game has been stopped for any reason other than those mentioned above.

The above mentioned fouls were prefaced with the words "outside the crease" which indicates that in this area there are special considerations, rules and privileges. For the attack player it places restrictions not to make it unfair, but as a protection for the goalkeeper. Though an attack player may run *through* the crease to field a wide ball, she may not have any part of her body or her crosse over the crease before, during or after a shot. No member of the attack may go within the crease to retrieve the ball, nor may any player check the goalkeeper while she is within the crease. Should there be any infringement of these rules, the goalkeeper is given a free position.

Now for rules of the crease in relation to the goalkeeper or any member of her team, and the special privileges of the goalkeeper. While within the crease, meaning that she *and* her crosse are in the crease, the goalkeeper may use her hand to stop a ball, to dislodge a ball should it be stuck in her crosse or in her pads. She must put the ball in her crosse and clear immediately. She must never just hold the ball in her crosse but must try to pass at once. The goalkeeper may draw the ball back into the crease as long as she has both feet in the crease. However, should she have one foot or both feet outside she may not step back in or run across the crease until she has passed the ball. Once outside the crease she loses her privilege of using her hands. Should she ever be outside the crease and another player has stepped into deputize for her, she may not return to her defending position until her teammate has left.

No defense player may carry the ball across the crease. For infringement of the rules of the crease by the defense, a free position is awarded to the attack, the place decided by the umpire. It must be ten yards from the goal and it will more often than not be behind the level of the goal line.

A goal is not counted if the ball enters the goal off the person of an attacking player.

The rules can be placed under the two headings of unfair and dangerous. With careful thought, you can interpret such situations should they occur and be quick to recognize them during a game. A good player knows the rules, for only then can she play intelligently and react accordingly.

Facts for Enthusiasts
and Unwritten Laws

Buy your own lacrosse stick if you possibly can. As no two crosses are exactly alike, it is important to have the grip and balance acceptable to you. To possess one provides more chance to practice on one's own. Practice not only those skills which give you pleasure because you have begun to master them, but more importantly, spend time on those that are not sufficiently a part of your "vocabulary."

To return to your crosse. Well-cared for, it will last a very long time. When you first purchase it, apply several coats of linseed oil to the wood and rub vaseline on all the rawhide and gut *except the guard and the bridge*—these two parts must not be softened. From then on, at the beginning and end of each season, one treatment should suffice unless you have played with your crosse in the rain, in which case after it has dried out, it should be oiled and lubricated. When not in use, store the crosse in a cool, dry place, properly hung on a hook from the upper corner of the crosse where the wood and guard meet. Store it where no mice can get to it; they love the rawhide particularly, also the gut.

When playing the game it is advisable to wear a thin, old pair of well fitting leather gloves. One's knuckles will occasionally get knocked and this layer of protection will help.

If you are a real enthusiast, a ball and a wall are all you need in order to practice, inside or outside. A friend to work with adds variety to the things it is possible to do. A lawn, a driveway, a quiet road or a beach can be used to great advantage in perfecting all the skills as well as providing marvellous exercise.

Playing in a team, of course, is the measure of your success. Your responsibility once this is achieved has now increased, both tangibly and intangibly. How you dress, how you react to situations both favorable and unfavorable, your relationship with your teammates, your attitude toward

68

your opponents, your manners and your appreciation for the umpires, must all be important personal concerns.

All members of a team should arrive well ahead of time for a game. Your appearance should be impeccable and you should all be dressed alike. Appearance is important both to you and to your team and also it affects the impression you will create. Time to warm up before a match is essential and your goalkeeper must be given primary consideration. A chance to move and to get her eye on the ball with *easy* shots at all levels will help to establish a very necessary confidence before the game gets underway.

It is part of the game's unwritten laws to shake hands and introduce yourself to your opponent, and at the end of a match to shake hands once again. If you are a member of the home team, your responsibility after the game is to look after your opponent during the social occasion which should follow the match.

During the game itself, you should be quietly guided by your captain. You have chosen her because you respect her knowledge and are willing to accept her advice. Her coaching will probably be at a minimum during actual play. An occasional quietly given caution or warning or even the high praise of "well done" might be heard. Otherwise, your game will be played in silence—a true test of your complete involvement, not only personal, but also as a member of the team—as you think and move together in harmony and understanding and in absolute concentration as you anticipate the moves of your opponents. The words "with you" may be used to advantage, when a teammate is having difficulty in finding a receiver for a pass, and you move quickly beside or behind her in readiness to help.

Your center umpire and your two goal umpires are there to control the game and to assist both teams to play advantageously. Your attitude toward them both during and following the game will be an indication of your manners and your appreciation.

On the east coast, in Pennsylvania, Vermont, Maine and Maryland there are resident hockey and lacrosse camps which run from the end of August through the first part of September, where you can go for concentrated coaching and playing. There are also some day camps with similar purposes. In all these situations you will not only have the chance to observe and be taught by players of top ability but you will also get to play with and against them. You may attend these camps regardless of your ability. Whatever this ability may be to begin with, you may be assured of a feeling of great accomplishment by the end of the session. Interest in the game and the desire to learn are the only prerequisites.

8

The Lore of Lacrosse

HISTORY

According to the *Encyclopedia Britannica*, lacrosse is the oldest organized sport in America, having been played by the Six Nations of the Iroquois throughout the Territory of New York State and lower Ontario before Columbus landed in the new world. "The Iroquois Confederation adopted the sport as a training measure for war." The game was taken up by white men about 1840 and became the national game of Canada.

Known by the Indians as "Baggataway" the present name came from a French missionary who called it La Crosse as the stick in the form then used reminded him of bishop's crozier. The name has since become all one word—lacrosse.

Records show that a team of Canadians played a team of Indians in England in 1867 in the presence of Queen Victoria.

It seems strange indeed that this game which began on our continent was *brought back to us as a sport for girls* by our English friends. Even in England it is a fairly recent game, as games go, but their ability to play it suggests it has been a part of their heritage for a much longer time. According to Margaret Boyd's book on lacrosse, some schools played matches as early as 1890 and 1891. Her book quotes the words of a head-mistress giving reasons why this sport was included in the curriculum of her school, ". . . qualities of combination, obedience, courage, individual unselfishness for the sake of the side—various kinds of skill required, fleetness of foot, quickness of eye, strength of wrist, and a great deal of judgement and knack. The game of lacrosse well played is a beautiful sight, the actions of the players so full of grace and agility. The skill required, moreover, is so great that the attempt to acquire it is a splendid training in courage and perseverance. . . ."

And so this sport for girls, as we know it, was born in England, and encouraged by educators who recognized its value. In the early 1900's teachers from England, then in some of our schools, introduced the game here. We in the States owe much to the late Mrs. Joyce Cran Barry who in the late twenties first introduced lacrosse at Wellesley College. Her ability, enthusiasm, knowledge and energy did much to spread the fun and worth-whileness of the game to many. In 1931, she was instrumental in forming the United States Women's Lacrosse Association and served as first president. That lacrosse isn't well known throughout our country can be attributed to several factors: the growth and popularity of hockey had captured the energies of players and teachers alike; schools and colleges have felt they could not afford to outfit students for both games; teachers have been hard to secure; some have felt there was no room in a program with tennis, softball, etc., already firmly established. The constant hope and interest of many people are directed toward solving these problems as soon as possible.

Many people both here and abroad have done much for the game, and to them, all who have ever played or will play must feel appreciation and gratitude. However, if names are mentioned, along with Mrs. Barry, the name of Margaret Boyd, player and teacher par excellence, must also be placed. The greatest single impact on our growth and improvement has come from her coaching of players and teachers of all abilities, since 1949. With enthusiasm ever-infectious, coaching indescribably successful, she has seen to fruition the development of many of our outstanding players, some of whom have gone on to become internationals, and she has encouraged and improved the play of hundreds of beginners.

In 1934 an unofficial English touring team arrived in America, intent upon teaching us how to play and to coach. In 1935 our first team went to England and returned determined to pass on what it had learned. One of the important concerns for every member of any touring team has been how to share with others her increased knowledge, her improvement and her good fortune.

In 1949 the first official English touring team visited the United States. In 1951, an American team paid a return visit; this was followed by another invitation to England to return here in 1954. When our next team crossed the Atlantic in 1957, and were once again so cordially and warmly entertained in England, Scotland, Ireland and Wales, the U.S.W.L.A. wanted to express its appreciation and gratitude. As the expense of having a touring team visit us every year is too prohibitive to be considered, a plan was evolved to invite a combined team composed of members of these various countries. So the idea of The Great Britain and Ireland Touring Team was conceived and invited to visit us in 1960. The G.B.I.T.T.'s, as they are affectionately known, returned here again in 1967 and in the meantime an American team went to the British Isles in 1964. Tours now take place every three or four years in one direction or the other. Though we have never defeated England, our team played a brilliant game and drew 7-7 in 1957.

Some lacrosse is played in Australia but unlike field hockey, a game known to most countries of the world, it is still largely unknown. Of interest is the difference in the playing seasons between our country and the British Isles. Whereas our game is usually considered a spring sport and played from the middle of March until the end of May, in the British Isles it is played from September to April.

With the superb coaching and help from our overseas friends, and because of the dedication and enthusiasm of many Americans, the number of people who have now been introduced to lacrosse has been greatly increased and our national level of skill has shown steady progress. Lacrosse has come a long way from its early beginnings of tribe against tribe to its trips across the Atlantic and back.

9

Playing Lacrosse

Those first people who formed the United States Women's Lacrosse Association must have felt what was expressed some years later by a President of the Association, "It is too grand a game to be enjoyed by so few."

The Association, completely amateur, is run by women who serve voluntarily in many different capacities helping (1) To introduce lacrosse throughout the country and to provide technical material, films, coaches and loan kits of equipment; (2) To improve the standard of play; (3) To provide competition at all levels. The U.S.W.L.A., therefore, is for you.

In the official *Field Hockey and Lacrosse Guide,* you will find not only information about the various committees and the contributions which are yours for the asking, but also the names of people to whom you may write to ask for information. The President of the Association will always welcome inquiries.

There is international competition whose thrill and opportunity must be the ambition of all keen players. Your immediate reaction must be: "How do I start on this road to the top?" When you leave school or college, lacrosse can still offer you opportunities for playing, for making new friends and, yes, even for travel! If club or association lacrosse is available where you live, your teacher should know this. If you move to a new area, write to the President or Secretary of the U.S.W.L.A. and ask what group you may join.

The National Association is made up of various Local Associations which have been created where there are enough players to form a fairly permanent nucleus, in which case appropriate teams are formed for practice and play. As sometimes the distance between local associations is too great for inter-season matches, the U.S.W.L.A. sponsors holiday week-ends, one northern and one southern. These are a source of delight for many reasons, not the least of which are meeting old friends and making new

Figure 27—Emblems

ones. People of varying abilities are mixed in their groupings and teams for stickwork practice and coached games; the week-end finishes with a tournament.

At the end of May or during the first part of June the lacrosse season is brought to its climax with a national tournament. Watching the play is a selection committee who choose the twelve individuals of The All American Lacrosse Team. The twelve next best are named as reserves. Should a tour be in the offing these players are given the first opportunity to go.

If you are chosen for a tour you are responsible for the expenses of your own uniform and travel, but when you arrive in a foreign country you become their guests. There is no better or easier way to become spoiled! Though expensive, it is a privilege no money can buy!

May this game, no matter on what level, bring to you an awareness of accomplishment, the joy and fun of competition in its finest form, an appreciation and understanding of this still "unknown" sport, and when you have finished your playing years may you reflect with a deep sense of satisfaction upon the pleasure that Lacrosse gave to you!

Excerpts from two newspaper accounts written for "The Times," London, by the late Mr. A. A. Thomson, a sports reporter, bring this text to a close. The author believes the reason for their inclusion is self-evident.

"The stranger, seeing his first Women's Lacrosse match, may afterwards feel he has been a little bemused by its speed and grace. Watching his second, in different conditions, his doubts fade, for again the vivid pattern is repeated and the rich kaleidoscope of colour and movement renews its swiftly changing rhythms . . .".

". . . . All games, if played with zest and skill, have their merits, but there is in Lacrosse a rhythm and felicity that can make other games look clumsy . . .".

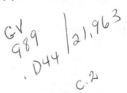

".... In this match the passing, catching and carrying followed shapes and rhythms of infinite variety . . .".

"Time and again, as an attack was mounted, it sprang creatively into a succession of ballet-like patterns varying and repeating themselves, but always making for goal . . .".

".... spontaneous vigour and sheer grace do not always blend: in the best of women's lacrosse they are happily married."

"Figures alone give no conception of the speed, the intensity and above all the patterned elegance of Lacrosse as a game."[1]

[1]This material is reproduced by permission of "The Times," London, from articles of March 6, 1967 and October 23, 1967.

Index